日 本 事 情
JAPAN à la carte

佐々木瑞枝 著

北星堂書店

ISBN 4-590-00783-5

序　文

　もう10年も前のことになるだろうか，私が教えていた外国人のための日本語クラスでこんな質問が出た。「先生，平仮名のヒラには何か意味がありますか？」「片仮名のカタはどうですか？」私は今でも背中を流れた冷たい汗の感触を思い出すことができる。そのクラスは大使館員，ビジネスマン，留学生などから成る「日本語上級クラス」だったが，皆非常に知識欲がおう盛で，時にはこちらがたじろぐような質問をぶつけてくるのだった。

　予想もつかない質問に備えて，私は自分で教材を準備することにした。生徒たちはその教材が気に入ったようで，日本の社会のさまざまな断面を教材にしてほしいという声が出た。そのころから書き出した教材用ノートが，この本の下敷になっている。

　ここ数年ケンブリッジで教えている「サマーコース日本語クラス」の外国人学生たちが，今の日本人の生活についてほとんど知識をもち合わせていない。そのこともまたこの本を出す一つのきっかけになった。彼らがこの本を読むことで，複雑で時には誤解されやすい日本の文化を，少しでも理解していただければと思う。

　この原稿を書くまでには，ずいぶん多くの方々や著書から教えを受けた。また英文については，J. D. Lamb 氏，C. Holmes 氏のお世話になった。心から感謝申し上げたい。随所に私の個人的な考え方が顔を出すと思うが，ご叱声いただければ幸いである。

1987年7月　　　　　　　　　　　　　　　　　　　　佐々木瑞枝

Preface

About ten years ago, I was teaching Japanese to a class of foreigners when I was asked the following question: "Does the hira in hiragana have any meaning? And what about the kata in katakana?" I can still remember the cold shiver that ran down my spine because I did not know the answer. It was an advanced class made up of diplomats, businessmen and full-time students, and I was often taken aback by the types of questions I came up against.

To better prepare myself for unexpected questions, I decided to start writing my own teaching materials. The students seemed to like them and requested that I prepare more on a wide range of facets of Japanese culture. The notes that I have been compiling since then form the foundation of this book.

During the past several summers of teaching Japanese in Cambridge, England, I've realized that many foreign students have little notion of contemporary Japanese life. As students progress through this book, I hope they will get some appreciation of how the traditional and the modern are combined in my complex and often little understood culture.

Many people helped me bring the manuscript to completion. I should like to express particular thanks to Mr. D. Lamb and Mr. C. Holmes for their translation. The opinions expressed herein are entirely my own.

July 1987   Mizue Sasaki

目　次

序文　Preface ……………………………………………………… iii

I. 日本の旅（スーザンの旅日記） …………………………… 2
Journey through Japan (Susan's Travel Diary)
1. 東　京　Tokyo ……………………………………………… 4
2. 九　州　Kyushu ……………………………………………… 6
3. 中　国　Chugoku …………………………………………… 10
4. 京　都　Kyoto ……………………………………………… 12
5. 奈　良　Nara ………………………………………………… 14
6. 東　北　Tohoku ……………………………………………… 16
7. 北海道　Hokkaido …………………………………………… 18
8. 旅を終えて　Impressions of the Journey ………………… 24

II. 日本の季節　Japanese Seasons ………………………… 26
1. 桜前線　The Cherry Blossom Front ……………………… 26
2. 入　梅　The Start of the Rainy Season ………………… 28
3. 真夏日　Hot Days of the Peak of Summer ……………… 28
4. 台　風　Typhoons …………………………………………… 30
5. 秋晴れ　Clear Days of Autumn …………………………… 30
6. 豪雪とブーゲンビリア　Heavy Snow and Bougainvilleas … 32

III. 年中行事　Annual Events and Seasonal Phenomena ……… 38
1. お正月　O-Shogatsu ………………………………………… 38
2. 成人の日　Adults Day ……………………………………… 40
3. 節　分　The Eve of Spring ………………………………… 40
4. ひな祭り　Hina Matsuri Dolls Festival …………………… 42
5. 入学式　Entrance Ceremonies ……………………………… 42
6. 子供の日・端午の節句　Children's Day, Boys' Festival …… 44
7. 七　夕　Tanabata, The Festival of the Weaver Star ……… 44

8. 七五三　Shichi-Go-San ……………………………………… *46*
　　9. 大みそか　O-Misoka ……………………………………… *46*

Ⅳ. 日本人の社会と生活 ……………………………………… *48*
　　　Japanese Society and the Life of the People
　　1. タテ社会　The Vertical Society ………………………… *48*
　　2. 恥の文化　Culture of Shame …………………………… *50*
　　3. 中流意識　Middle Class Consciousness ……………… *52*
　　4. 年功序列　Seniority Rule ………………………………… *54*
　　5. 学歴偏重社会 ……………………………………………… *56*
　　　The Over-emphasis on Educational Background
　　6. 単身赴任　Single Posting ………………………………… *60*
　　7. 勤務時間と休暇　Work and Leisure …………………… *64*
　　8. 日本の宗教　Japanese Religion ………………………… *66*
　　9. 男女雇用機会均等法　Equal Opportunities for Women …… *70*
　　10. 見合い結婚　Arranged Marriages ……………………… *72*
　　11. 安全・確実な日本の社会　A Safe and Stable Society ……… *74*

Ⅴ. 日本の文化　Japanese Cultural Activities …………………… *78*
　　1. 日本の音楽　Japanese Music …………………………… *78*
　　2. 能と狂言　Noh and Kyogen …………………………… *82*
　　3. 歌舞伎　Kabuki ………………………………………… *88*
　　4. 着　物　Kimono ………………………………………… *92*
　　5. 茶の湯　The Tea Ceremony …………………………… *96*
　　6. 生け花　The Art of Flower Arrangement …………… *98*
　　7. 盆　栽　Miniature Trees ……………………………… *102*
　　8. カタカナ・ひらがな　Katakana and Hiragana ………… *106*
　　9. 百人一首 …………………………………………………… *108*
　　　One Hundred Poems by One Hundred Poets
　　10. 俳　句　Haiku …………………………………………… *112*
　　11. 書　道　Calligraphy …………………………………… *116*

- 12. やきもの　Pottery and Ceramics ……………………………… *118*
- Ⅵ. スポーツ　Sports …………………………………………………… *124*
  - 1. 相　撲　Sumo ………………………………………………… *124*
  - 2. 柔　道　Judo ………………………………………………… *130*
  - 3. 野　球　Baseball …………………………………………… *132*
- Ⅶ. 日本歴史の旅　Journey through Japanese History ………… *136*
  - 1. 原始社会　Primitive Society ……………………………… *136*
  - 2. 古代社会初期　Beginning of Ancient Society ………… *138*
  - 3. 律令社会　Society Based on Law ……………………… *140*
  - 4. 貴族社会　Aristocratic Society ………………………… *144*
  - 5. 封建社会の成立　Establishment of Feudal Society ……… *146*
  - 6. 封建社会の完成　Consummation of Feudal Society ……… *150*
  - 7. 近代日本の成立　Modern Japan ………………………… *158*
  - 8. 二度の世界大戦　The Two World Wars ……………… *164*
  - 9. 新しい日本　The New Japan …………………………… *166*
- Ⅷ. 日本の文学　Aspects of Japanese Literature ……………… *170*
  - 1. 万葉集　Manyoshu ………………………………………… *170*
  - 2. 枕草子　Makura no Soshi ………………………………… *174*
  - 3. 源氏物語　Genji Monogatari ……………………………… *176*
  - 4. 平家物語　Heike Monogatari …………………………… *178*
  - 5. 日本永代蔵　Nihon Eitai Gura …………………………… *182*
  - 6. 奥の細道　Oku no Hosomichi …………………………… *184*
  - 7. 夏目漱石　Natsume Soseki ……………………………… *186*
  - 8. 芥川竜之介　Akutagawa Ryunosuke …………………… *190*
  - 9. 川端康成　Kawabata Yasunari …………………………… *192*
  - 10. 谷崎潤一郎　Tanizaki Jun'ichiro ………………………… *194*
  - 11. 三島由紀夫　Mishima Yukio ……………………………… *198*
- Ⅸ. 日本経済の特質 ……………………………………………………… *202*
  Characteristics of the Japanese Economy

1.	高度成長　High-speed Growth	202
2.	中小企業　The Small- and Medium-Sized Businesses	204
3.	農業と食糧の問題　Agriculture and Food	206
4.	漁　業　Fishing Industry	208

X. コンピュータ　Computer ………………………………………… 212
   1. コンピュータ社会　Computer Society …………………… 212
   2. ソフトウェア，ハードウェア　Software and Hardware …… 216
   3. IBM と日本製コンピュータ ……………………………………… 218
      IBM and Japanese Computers
   4. コンピュータとプライバシー　Computers and Privacy …… 220

XI. ロボット　Robots ……………………………………………………… 224
   1. 産業用ロボット　Industrial Robots ……………………………… 224
   2. ロボット導入のよいこと，悪いこと ……………………………… 226
      Robots Good and Bad
   3. 中小企業とロボット …………………………………………………… 228
      Robots in Small- and Medium-sized Businesses
   4. ロボットの種類と用途 ………………………………………………… 230
      Varieties of Robots and Their Applications

viii 目 次

日　本　事　情

JAPAN à la carte

I. 日本の旅 (スーザンの旅日記)

　こんにちは，私は スーザン，メルボルン大学の学生，20歳です。今度，かねてからの *憧れの国，日本へ行きます。3週間で日本全国を一周してみようと思います。ちょっと忙しい旅になるかもしれないけれど，できるだけ *欲ばって日本を見てくるつもりです。

　日本では交通費がとてもかかるそうなのでオーストラリアで Japan Rail Pass[1] を買っていくことにしました。このパスさえあれば日本のJR線に *乗り放題，それに急行や新幹線にまで乗れるので，交通費がだいぶ *節約できそうです。その分おいしいものが食べられるかな？

VOCABULARY　　*Akogare:* longing, yearning for　　*Yokubaru:* be greedy, covetous (for)　　*Norihodai:* travel as much as one likes　　*Setsuyaku suru:* economise

【参考】

	自由席新幹線	グリーン席
東京—博多	20,200	28,000

The standard fare from Tokyo to Hakata (return) by bullet train is ¥40,400.

I. Journey through Japan (Susan's Travel Diary)

Hello, I'm Susan. I'm a student at Melbourne University and I'm twenty years old. I'm off to Japan, a country I have always longed to visit. I want to try to travel around the whole country in three weeks. It will probably be a rather hectic journey but I intend to see as much of the country as I can.

I hear that travel is very expensive in Japan so I have decided to buy a Japan Rail Pass before leaving Australia. If you have one you can travel as much as you like on the Japan Railways, even on express and Bullet trains. It looks as if I'll be able to save quite a lot in travelling expenses and perhaps I'll be able to spend more on nice things to eat.

NOTES

1.

Japan Rail Pass	GREEN		ORDINARY	
	Adults	Children	Adults	Children
7–DAY	¥37,000	¥18,500	¥27,000	¥13,500
14–DAY	60,000	30,000	43,000	21,500
21–DAY	78,000	39,000	55,000	27,500

1. 東　京

4月1日

　成田空港に到着，東京に向かう。オーストラリアとは，*時差が1時間しかないので楽。その点，ヨーロッパから来た人は大変でしょうね。

　飯田橋の国際ユースホステルに泊まる。とても清潔だし部屋のデザインもよい。窓からはお*堀が見える。

　部屋に荷物を置いて原宿へ。平日だというのに人が多いのに驚く。どの通りも若い人でいっぱいだ。日本の学校は春休み中だと聞いて納得がいく。

　明治神宮はさすがに静かで*神秘的な空気が漂っている。東京には緑が少ないと聞いていたけれど，ここは数少ない緑の一つかしら。

　夜は日本人の友達に案内されて新宿の副都心へ。高層ビル群が立ち並んでいる。地震の時は大丈夫なのかしら。50階から見た東京は光の渦でとても美しい。

VOCABULARY　　*Jisa*: time difference, lag　　*Hori*: moat
Shimpiteki: mysterious

4月2日

　きょうは地下鉄の一日切符を買ってあちこち歩いた。浅草の浅草寺（せんそうじ），上野の美術館。上野公園の桜はあと4～5日で咲き始めるとのこと。

1. Tokyo

April 1

Arrived at Narita and then went in to Tokyo. The time lag between Australia and Japan is only one hour so there was no problem. In that respect it must be difficult for people coming from Europe.

Am staying at the International Youth Hostel in Iidabashi. It's very clean and the rooms are nicely designed. From the window I can see the moat of the Imperial Palace.

Left my baggage in my room and went to Harajuku. I was amazed at the crowds, even on a weekday. Every street was full of young people. I understood why when I was told that schools in Japan are now in the spring vacation.

As you would expect, Meiji Jingu was peaceful and had an air of mystery about it. I had heard there was little greenery in Tokyo but this must be one of the exceptions.

In the evening I was taken by a Japanese friend to see Shinjuku, one of the town centres. A mass of tall buildings, I wonder if they are safe in earthquakes. From the fiftieth floor, Tokyo was a beautiful whirlpool of lights.

April 2

Today I bought a one day pass on the subway and walked about here and there. Saw the Sensoji Temple at Asakusa and the Ueno Art Gallery. The cherry blossoms in Ueno Park

*国会議事堂から丸の内の*官庁街，このへんが日本の心臓部，大手町ではビジネスマンでいっぱいの食堂でてんぷらを食べた。700円。ランチタイムは特に安いそうだ。

　午後は秋葉原の*電器街へ。どの店にもステレオ，テレビ，ビデオがある。セールスマンが*街頭で叫び，音楽がやかましい。子供たちが夢中になってコンピュータゲームをしている。ここでは定価の3割から4割引きという。私も何か買いたかったけれど，日本は100ボルトということなのでやめにした。しかし街全部が電器屋さんというのは壮観だった。

VOCABULARY　　*Kokkaigijido:* National Diet Building　　*Kanchogai:* area of ministerial buildings　　*Denkigai:* Electric goods area　　*Gaito:* the street

2. 九　州

4月3日

　朝，新幹線ひかり号で博多に向かう。東京から7時間の*快適な旅だった。

　福岡県にあるこの街の中央を流れる那珂川の東が博多，西が福岡で，近代都市の福岡と歴史的な街の博多が*一体になっている。

　博多駅からバスで35分，太宰府へ。駅前でレンタサイクルを借り天満宮を訪れた。

VOCABULARY　　*Kaiteki:* agreeable, pleasant　　*Ittai ni naru:* become as one

6　I. 日本の旅

will be out in four or five days' time.

From the National Diet I went to Marunouchi where the government ministries are located. Ate tempura in a restaurant full of business men. ¥700. Apparently it's very cheap at lunch time.

Went to Akihabara, the electrical goods district, in the afternoon. Stereos, televisions and videos everywhere. Salesmen shouting in the streets and music playing full blast. Children engrossed in computer games, oblivious to everything. Prices here are 30–40% lower than normal. I wanted to buy something but decided not to because everything in Japan is 100 volts. But it was impressive seeing a whole district of nothing but electrical stores.

2. Kyushu

April 3

Took the Hikari Bullet Train to Hakata. It was a comfortable seven-hour journey from Tokyo.

The town is located in Fukuoka Prefecture. The River Naka flows through the middle so that Hakata lies to the east and Fukuoka to the west. In this way, the modern city Fukuoka and historical Hakata become one.

Then to Dazaifu, thirty-five minutes from Hakata by bus. Hired a bicycle outside the station and visited the Tenmangu Shrine.

4月4日

　急行「かもめ」で長崎へ。

　鎖国時代¹, 海外に対して開かれた*唯一の街だった。長崎駅から市電でオランダ坂へ。*石畳と坂道の多いこの街は歩くのが一番よい。「浦上」には*原爆の資料が展示されていて*胸が痛んだ。

VOCABULARY　*Yuiitsu:* unique　　*Ishidatami:* stone pavement
Genbaku (Genshibakudan): atom bomb　　*Mune ga itamu:* be grieved, troubled

注
1. 鎖国時代
　16世紀, 日本にキリスト教が伝わり, 信者の数が増えていった。ヨーロッパの強大な勢力の進出を恐れた当時の為政者たちは, 鎖国政策をとって, 国民の海外渡航さえ禁じた。

4月5日

　定期観光バスに乗って雲仙, 島原, 天草, 熊本を見て阿蘇¹に着いた。約10時間の長い旅だったが, *雄大な景色を楽しむことができた。バスの中では皆と下手な日本語で話して友達もたくさんできた。

VOCABULARY　*Yudai na:* majestic, grand, sublime

注
1. 阿蘇
　世界の中でもスケールの大きい活火山で, 現在も噴火を続けている。

April 4

Took the "Kamome" Express to Nagasaki.

During the period of national isolation, this was the only town open to the rest of the world. Took the street car from Nagasaki Station to Orandazaka (Dutch Hill). With its many sloping and paved streets, it is best to see this area on foot. I was upset after seeing the atomic bomb exhibition at Uragami.

NOTES

1. Christianity was introduced into Japan in the sixteenth century and the number of converts increased. Many statesmen feared the encroachment of the great European powers, so they adopted the isolation policy and forbade the people to go abroad.

April 5

Went on a guided bus tour to Aso via Unzen, Shimabara, Amakusa and Kumamoto. A long journey of about ten hours but enjoyed some superb scenery. Was able to practise my clumsy Japanese on the bus and made a lot of friends.

NOTES

1. Mt. Aso ranks as one of the largest active volcanoes in the world with eruptions still occurring frequently.

3. 中 国

4月6日 (広島, 宮島)

　九州は北九州を回った。今度日本に来る時のために, 南九州と沖縄は残しておこう。

　博多から新幹線で広島へ。原爆を受けた都市, 広島は観光地というにはあまりに*悲惨だ。平和記念公園では平和について考える貴重なひとときを過ごした。

　夕方宮島へ。海の中に立つ赤い*大鳥居, 本殿, *国宝だけあって見事な社殿だ。

VOCABULARY　　*Hisan:* wretched　　*O-Torii:* Great torii gate　*Kokuho:* National Treasure

4月7日 (姫路)

　*途中下車をして姫路城を見学, 17世紀に完成したこの*優雅な城は, 白鷺城とも呼ばれているそうだ。城内を見学するのに*たっぷり2時間はかかった。城の中には家具というものがほとんどない。昔の人はどうやって生活したのだろうか。

VOCABULARY　　*Tochu gesha:* break a (train) journey　　*Yuga:* refinement, elegance　　*Tappuri:* to the full, a good (two hours)

4月8日 (姫路, 倉敷)

　倉敷では, 大原美術館や倉敷美術館など, 一日ではとても見て回れないほどの絵画や彫刻, 世界の一流品がこの小さな*一角に集まっている。美観地区と呼ばれる一角は土蔵と倉屋敷の白い壁

3. Chugoku

April 6 (Hiroshima, Miyajima)

What I saw of Kyushu was all in the north. I left South Kyushu and Okinawa until my next visit to Japan.

Went by Bullet Train from Hakata to Hiroshima. To have become a sightseeing attraction because of the atomic bombing is tragic. Spent a worthwhile time in the Peace Memorial Park thinking about peace.

In the evening to Miyajima. As was to be expected from a shrine designated a National Treasure, the red torii gates in the sea and the main sanctuary were magnificent.

April 7 (Himeji)

I broke a journey to see Himeji Castle. Completed in the seventeenth century, this graceful and elegant building is also called the White Crane Castle. It took all of two hours to see the interior. As there was little furniture in evidence, I wonder how people lived in those days.

April 8 (Himeji, Kurashiki)

In Kurashiki, at the Ohara and Kurashiki Museums there were so many first class paintings and sculptures from all over the world that one day is not enough to see the large number that have been collected together in this small area. In

が立ち並び，お堀には柳の影が写っている。向こうからサムライが歩いて来たとしても，ちっとも驚かないだろう。

VOCABULARY　　*Ikkaku:* a corner

4. 京　都

4月9日

　いよいよ京都に到着。オーストラリアにいる時からたくさんの写真を見てきたので，どこに行ってよいのか迷うほどだ。やはり最初は桂離宮に行こう。

4月10日（洛西）

　次は金閣寺。三層の楼閣が金色に輝き，池にその影を写している。

　ここから少し*足を伸ばして*石庭で有名な竜安寺へ。

　長方形の庭に敷かれた白い砂，砂には円と直線が描かれ15個の石が置かれただけの*簡素な庭，苦いお抹茶[1]をいただきながら庭を眺める。しばらくこれを眺めていたら，海と島に見えてくるのかしら。

　夕食は嵐山の渡月橋の近くで和食をいただいた。緑の中に桜が美しい。

VOCABULARY　　*Ashi o nobasu:* go, walk as far as...　　*Sekitei:* rock, stone garden　　*Kanso:* simplicity

one part of the town, regarded as a great beauty spot, there are rows of white walled storage and warehouses and willow trees are reflected in the waters of the canals. I wouldn't have been surprised to see samurai warriors walking along.

4. Kyoto

April 9

I have arrived in Kyoto at last. But, having seen so many photographs in Australia, I just don't know where to start. I think I'll go to the Katsura Detached Palace first.

April 10 (The Western Part of the City)

The next place I visited was Kinkakuji Temple. Its three gleaming gold roofs were reflected in the lake beside it.

From there it was a good walk to Ryoanji Temple with its famous stone garden.

Rectangular in shape and spread with sand which has been swept into lines and circles, the garden is very simple with fifteen rocks placed in it. Drinking bitter mattcha tea, I contemplated the garden and wondered if it would turn into a group of islands surrounded by sea if I were to look long enough.

In the evening had a Japanese-style dinner at Arashiyama

注―――――――――
 1. 抹茶
   摘みとった茶の芽を粉末としたもの。湯を注ぎ，かきまぜて飲む。

4月11日（洛北(らくほく)）

 バスを降りて坂道を上る。細い道の両側のつけもの屋さんや*民芸品の店を*冷やかしながら行くと三千院(さんぜんいん)に出る。高い杉木立，*こけむした庭，*読経(どきょう)の声，ここは宗教的な静けさに満ちている。

VOCABULARY　*Mingeihin:* folk crafts　*Hiyakasu:* window-shop　*Kokemusu:* be overgrown with moss　*Dokkyo:* chanting Buddhist sutras, scriptures

5. 奈　良

4月12日

 京都から奈良に*立ち寄った。奈良は京都とともに，戦争の被害を受けていないということで，*古代の*舞台装置を見ているような気がする。

 奈良駅からバスで東大寺(とうだいじ)へ。奈良は*修学旅行の*メッカだそうで，黒い制服を着た高校生たちが*ぞろぞろ歩いている。世界一大きい木造建築といわれる*大仏殿で大仏様を見る。なにしろ大きい。手の平に人間が10人ほど乗れそうだ。大きいけれど，優しい顔をしている。

 奈良に来たら，やはりシカに会っていこうと奈良公園へ。約

14　I．日本の旅

close to the Togetsukyō Bridge. The cherry blossoms were beautiful amongst all the greenery.

NOTES

1. *Mattcha*: Powdered, whipped green tea used in tea ceremony.

April 11 (The Northern Part of the City)

Alighted from the bus and climbed a narrow road up a hill. Looked in the pickle and folk craft shops on either side before coming to Sanzen-in Temple. With its groves of tall cryptomerias, moss-covered garden and the sound of voices, chanting sutras, the whole area was imbued with a sense of religious calm.

5. Nara

April 12

Left Kyoto to take a look at Nara. Like Kyoto, Nara was not damaged by bombing during the war so I felt as if I was looking at the scenery of some drama set in ancient times.

Then by bus from Nara Station to the Todaiji Temple. Nara is apparently the mecca for school excursions so the temple was swarming with high school students dressed in their black uniforms. Saw the giant Buddha of Todaiji housed in what is said to be the biggest wooden building in the world. Anyway, the statue is certainly gigantic. Ten people can stand

1000頭もいる シカが*人なつこく寄ってくる。シカの主食は公園の芝だそうで，これなら*手がかからなくていい。メスが7割ということで，ここは*女性上位かしら。シカと遊んでから夕方東京へ。

VOCABULARY　　*Tachiyoru:* stop by at, drop in on　　*Kodai no:* ancient, classical　　*Butai sochi:* (stage) setting, scenery　　*Shugaku ryoko:* school outing, excursion　　*Mekka:* mecca　　*Zorozoro:* in succession, one after the other　　*Daibutsuden:* Great Hall of the Buddha　　*Hitonatsukoi:* tame　　*Te ga kakaru:* involve a lot of work, trouble　　*Joseijoi:* women are superior in rank

6. 東 北

4月13日

朝，上野から東北新幹線で岩手県の盛岡に行く。わずか3時間20分，東北新幹線が*開通したのは1985年3月，以前は盛岡まで6時間かかったとか。私は開通したあと日本に来て*運がよかったわ。

東北も見たい所は多いけれど，今回はあきらめて北海道に*直行することにした。青森より青函連絡船で函館へ（3時間50分）。JRパスはフェリーにも使えるから大変便利だ。

VOCABULARY　　*Kaitsu suru:* open to traffic, open a railway　　*Un ga yoi:* be fortunate, fortunately　　*Chokko:* direct (to), through (train)

in the palm of its hand. Despite its size, its face has a gentle expression.

Having come all the way to Nara, I could not very well leave without seeing the deer so I went to Nara Park where there are about a thousand and all so tame. They come right up to people. The deer live mainly on the grass in the park and, as long as they get enough, they can be left alone. Seventy percent of the deer are females, I hear. I wonder if that means the females are in charge. Having seen the deer, I returned to Tokyo.

6. Tohoku

April 13

In the morning took the Tohoku Bullet Train from Ueno to Morioka in Iwate Prefecture. The journey was only three hours and twenty minutes. The Tohoku Bullet Train began operating in March, 1985. Before that it took six hours to get to Morioka. Thank goodness I came to Japan after the line opened.

There are many places I want to visit in Tohoku but I resigned myself to not seeing them this time and went straight on to Hokkaido. Took the Seikan Boat Connection from Aomori to Hakodate (3 hours 50 minutes). The JR pass is very useful because you can use it on ferries as well.

7. 北海道

4月14日 (函館)

　北海道の*玄関口，函館に着いた。朝6時だというのに，とてもにぎやかだ。どうも*朝市のせいらしい。マーケットには，サケ，*海草，*するめ，とれたばかりのカニなどが売られていた。いかにも北の港町らしい。

　夜はロープウェイで函館山に登った。*夜景がとても美しかった。

VOCABULARY　　*Genkanguchi:* gateway　　*Asaichi:* (early) morning market　　*Kaiso:* (edible) seaweed　　*Surume:* dried cuttlefish　　*Yakei:* night view

4月15日 (大沼国定公園)

　函館から函館本線に乗って大沼公園へ。湖に浮かぶ小さな緑の島々と駒が岳の姿を映す沼。いつまで眺めていてもあきないほど美しい。

4月16日 (札幌)

　急行で4時間50分，札幌に着いた。高層ビルが建ち並び，地下鉄が走っている近代的な街だ。2月は雪まつりが催されるという大通り公園も，雪はすっかり溶けてしまっている。

　ホテルを捜していたら，「よかったら，私の家に泊まってください」と招待された。お金も残り少ないので，喜んでお受けする。

7. Hokkaido

April 14 (Hakodate)

Arrived in Hakodate, the gateway to Hokkaido. Although it was only six o'clock in the morning, it seemed to be a very busy place. This was probably because of the early morning market where salmon, edible seaweed, dried cuttlefish and freshly caught crab were on sale. A typical northern harbour town.

At night I went to the top of Mt. Hakodate by ropeway. The view was very beautiful.

April 15 (Onuma National Park)

Took the Hakodate Line from Hakodate to Onuma Park, a beautiful area of lakes and marshes with tree-covered islands and Mt. Komagatake reflected in the water. It was impossible to tire of such a sight.

April 16 (Sapporo)

Went by express train to Sapporo in 4 hours 50 minutes. Sapporo is a modern city with tall buildings and a subway system. In February a snow festival is held in the central Odori Park but by now the snow had all melted.

While I was looking for a hotel, someone invited me to stay at his house. As I was running out of money, I was

その人は木村さんといってラーメン屋さん。奥さんと2人でお店を経営しているということで、店の2階に畳の部屋が2つあった。時々外国人のお客さんがラーメンを食べに来ると泊めてあげるそうだ。「英会話の練習になりますから」と言っていた。*当然夕食はラーメン。スープがとてもおいしかった。

VOCABULARY　　*Tozen:* natural, a matter of course

4月17日
　もう一日、木村さんの家に泊めていただき、今日は札幌の街を見学した。

4月18日（旭川）
　朝早く札幌を*たち旭川へ。ここからバスで層雲峡へ向かう。日本一の*大峡谷という*名に恥じない*絶壁が24kmにわたって続いている。旭川駅から急行バスで1時間40分かかる。夜は*温泉旅館に泊まった。

VOCABULARY　　*Tatsu:* depart, set off　　*Daikyokoku:* (large) ravine, canyon　　*Na ni haji nai:* can be called without exaggeration　　*Zeppeki:* precipice, cliff face　　*Onsen ryokan:* traditional Japanese style inn with hot water tapped direct from a natural spring

4月19日（洞爺）
　このあと網走、阿寒と足を伸ばしたかったが、パスの*期限はあと2日だ。それまでに東京に戻らなければならない。Uターンして、室蘭本線に乗り、洞爺に向かう。
　洞爺湖は周囲43キロの湖。ここは北海道では珍しく、冬も凍ら

happy to accept.

He turned out to be a Mr. Kimura who is married with two children and runs a ramen shop. Upstairs he has two rooms and he sometimes puts foreigners up for the night who come to eat at his shop. He said it was so that he could practice his English. Not surprisingly, the ramen soup we had with the dinner was delicious.

April 17

Stayed one more day with Mr. Kimura and looked around the town.

April 18 (Asahikawa)

Left Sapporo early this morning and went to Asahikawa. Then took a bus to Sounkyo which can be called without exaggeration, the deepest canyon in Japan the walls of which extend for more than 24 kilometres. It is about 1 hour and 40 minutes from Asahikawa Station by express bus. Stayed the night at a hot spring inn.

April 19 (Toya)

I had hoped to go as far as Abashiri and Akan but my pass expires in two days by which time I have to be back in Tokyo. I made a U-turn here and headed for Toya by the main Muroran Line.

Lake Toya has a circumference of about 43 kilometres.

ない湖だそうだ。

洞爺湖のすぐそばには，火山の昭和新山がある。もと畑だったところが爆発*を重ね*2年がかりでできた新しい火山だ。私がこの次，日本に来る時は，この山はもっと高くなっているかもしれない。だって今も激しく活動しているのだから。現在の高さは標高407メートルだ。

VOCABULARY　　*Kigen:* period of time, time limit　　*...o kasaneru:* repeat　　*Ninen gakari:* over two years, taking two years

4月20日（函館）

洞爺湖から急行バスに乗り函館に着く。フェリーの出るまで4時間あり，おすしを食べて待つ。初めは生の魚が食べられなかったけれど，日本を旅行するうちに，だんだんおいしいと感じるようになった。人間の*味覚も変わるものだと*内心驚く。今晩は青森に泊まる。

VOCABULARY　　*Mikaku:* sense of taste, palate　　*Naishin:* inwardly, secretly

4月21日

朝起きると*聞き慣れないことばが聞こえてくる。これが東北弁というのだろう。今度の旅行で，少ししか日本語の分からない私にも，日本にはたくさんの方言があることを知った。でも皆私には標準語でゆっくり話しかけてくれる。早く日本語が覚えたいわ。

きょうでJRパスも終わり。日本*駆け歩きの忙しい旅だったけれど，あちこちで日本人に親切にされ，とても楽しい旅行だった。今度日本に来る時は，一年くらいの予定でゆっくり見て回り

Apparently it does not freeze over in winter which is unusual for Hokkaido.

Close to Lake Toya is the Showashinzan Volcano. It is a new volcano that formed in just over two years, after repeated eruptions in an area that was formerly just fields. As the volcano is still active, it will probably be even higher by the time I next come to Japan. At the moment its height is about 407 metres.

April 20 (Hakodate)

Took the express bus from Lake Toya and arrived in Hakodate. With four hours to wait for the ferry, I had some sushi to eat. The first time I tried raw fish I couldn't eat it but since travelling through Japan I have gradually come to find it delicious. Inwardly I am amazed that one's sense of taste can also change. This evening I am staying in Aomori.

April 21

When I got up this morning, I could hear voices speaking in the strange Tohoku dialect. Although I know only a little Japanese, this journey has made me realise that there are many dialects in Japan. But when people speak to me, they do so slowly, using the standard pronunciation. I do want to learn Japanese quickly.

Today my rail pass expired. My journey around Japan was rather rushed but I enjoyed it very much and people

たい。

　お昼の東北新幹線で盛岡より，東京へ。夕方，東京に着いた。

VOCABULARY　　*Kikinarenai:* strange, unfamiliar, unaccustomed to hearing　　*Kakearuku:* walk, journey at a fast rate

8.　旅を終えて

4月22日

　日本は小さい国だと思っていたが，3週間かけても見残したものがたくさんある。今度は留学生として日本に来て，1～2年日本に滞在したい。そうすれば，日本をもっと深く知ることができるだろうから。

　地方に行くと，風のにおいや人々の表情までが*なごやかに感じられた。これが世界中に製品を*売りまくっている日本人と同じ民族なのだろうか？

　それにこの旅行で，日本の長い歴史を*肌で感じることができたのも，一つの収穫だった。日本人は歴史を大切に受け継ぎながら，新しく発展を続けている……そんな印象を私は受けたが，当たっているだろうか。今度日本に来る時は，もっと日本語を勉強して，たくさんの人と友達になりたいと思う。

VOCABULARY　　*Nagoyaka:* genial, amiable, agreeable　　*Urimakuru:* sell furiously　　*Hada de kanjiru:* get the feel of, experience at first hand

everywhere were very kind. The next time I come to Japan I want to spend a year seeing the country properly.

At midday I took the Tohoku Bullet Train from Morioka and arrived in Tokyo in the evening.

8. Impressions of the Journey

April 22

I had thought that Japan was a small country but, even though I spent three weeks travelling, there were still many places that I had to miss out. Next time, I want to come as a foreign student and stay for one or two years. In that way I shall be able to get to know Japan in greater depth.

By travelling to different regions I was able to see the country and the people at close quarters in a most agreeable way. I could not help wondering whether the Japanese I met were of the same stock as those who are frantically marketing this country's products the world over.

Another benefit of my journey was being able to get the feel for Japan's long history. I had the impression that the Japanese value their history yet, at the same time, they are very progressive. I wonder if I am right about that. Anyhow, the next time I come to Japan, I want to study the language more and make friends with many people.

Ⅱ. 日本の季節

1. 桜前線

　地形が複雑で細長い日本列島は，桜の咲く日がだいぶ違います。桜前線（桜の花が咲き始める日と，場所をつなげた線）をよく調べておかなくてはいけません。

　ソメイヨシノ[1]は九州や四国の南では3月の終わりにはもう咲くそうです。でも北海道では5月になってやっと咲き始めます。2か月も違いがあるのには驚かされます。桜の花を追いかけて日本を旅行するとちょうど2か月かかることになります。今度そんな旅行をしてみるのはどうでしょうか。

　富士山に咲くのはヤマザクラ[2]。100メートル上がるごとに開花は3日遅れるそうです。桜前線は山のふもとから山頂に上がっていきます。薄いピンクが下から少しずつ山を染めていき，想像しただけですばらしいです。

II. Japanese Seasons

1. The Cherry Blossom Front

As the topography of the long and narrow Japanese archipelago is so complicated, the day when the cherry trees come into bloom can vary tremendously. You have to check the Cherry Blossom Front (a line showing the day the cherry blossoms appear and the location) very carefully.

In Kyushu and southern Shikoku, the Somei Yoshino is apparently already in bloom at the end of March. But in Hokkaido the blossoms do not appear until May. This two-month difference is truly amazing. In other words if you want to travel the length of Japan following the cherry blossoms, the journey will take exactly two months. Wouldn't you like to make that journey next time.

The cherry trees that flower on Mt. Fuji are called Yamazakura. It seems that for every 100 meters you go up, the blossoms appear three days later. So the Sakura Zensen starts at the bottom of the mountain and works its way up to the peak. It's wonderful just to imagine the pale pink that gradually colours the mountain from the bottom to the top.

注───────────────────────────
1. ソメイヨシノ
   葉の出る前にピンクで5弁の花が枝いっぱいに咲く。桜の代表ともいえるもの。
2. ヤマザクラ
   古い時代から日本の代表的な桜で，山地に広く自生し，また植えられている。奈良県の吉野山が有名。

2. 入　梅

　6月10日ごろから約1か月，梅雨の季節に入ります。梅の実が熟れるころなので梅雨というのでしょう。毎日のように雨が降り続きうっとうしい季節です。農家の人にとっては，田植えをする時季です。

3. 真夏日

　8月は真夏日が続きます。真夏日とは平均気温が30度以上の日です。
　日本では北の札幌の真夏日が9日ぐらいしかないのに対して，南の九州では60日前後も真夏日が続きます。東京では約45日，京都は盆地にあるため空気のとおりが悪く約68日も続きます。日本の夏は気温が高いだけでなく，湿度も高いので，不快に感じる人が多いのです。

NOTES
1. *Somei Yoshino*: Before the leaves appear, the branches are covered in pink, five-petalled blossom. Can be called the typical cherry blossom.
2. *Yamazakura*: From ancient times, the representative Japanese cherry. It grows wild and is also cultivated. Mt. Yoshino in Nara Prefecture is famous for them.

2. The Start of the Rainy Season

The rainy season begins around June 10 and lasts approximately one month. Because it is the time when plum trees ripen, this season is also called tsuyu or "plum rain". With rain falling for days on end it is a gloomy period but for farmers it is the time when they plant their rice.

3. Hot Days of the Peak of Summer

In August the hot days of the peak of summer (Manatsubi) continue. Manatsubi refers to the period when temperatures exceed 30 degrees for days on end.

In Japan, Manatsubi can be as short as about nine days in Sapporo in the north. In contrast, in Kyushu in the south it can extend to almost sixty days. In Tokyo it lasts for about forty-five days and in Kyoto, because the city is located in a valley

4. 台　風

　台風は9月の始めごろから，毎年のように日本を襲い，大きい災害を与えます。暴風雨で水害などが引き起こされ，床上浸水する家もあり，畳を干したり後始末が大変です。また台風のあと，野菜や魚類が必ず値上がりするので，台風の情報が入ったら，少し買いだめしておくことです。

5. 秋晴れ

　10月になると，蒸し暑い日が去り，気温も下がり，湿度も少なくなって秋晴れの日が続きます。明け方の気温が8度から9度ぐらいになると木々は紅葉し始めます。もみじは10月上旬に北海道で始まり，11月中旬～下旬に東京に達します。桜前線とはちょうど正反対の進み方です。

and the air is sluggish, for about sixty-eight. In Japan, the summer is not just a question of high temperatures, there is also much humidity which many people find unpleasant.

4. Typhoons

Around the beginning of September, Japan is annually visited by typhoons and the results can be disastrous. Heavy rains cause much damage and when houses are inundated and floors under water, the subsequent process of drying out the tatami mats involves much hard work. In addition, prices of vegetables and fish always go up after a typhoon. When a typhoon is announced, therefore, it is advisable to stock up quickly.

5. Clear Days of Autumn

In October, humidity decreases, temperatures drop and the clear days of autumn begin. When dawn temperatures reach eight or nine degrees, trees begin to display their autumn colours (Koyo). This process begins in Hokkaido in early October and reaches Tokyo by mid or late November. The direction is exactly the opposite of the Cherry Blossom Front.

6. 豪雪とブーゲンビリア

　日本列島の北端から南端までは3000kmある。だから南と北では温度差が大変大きい。
　2月，富山県に住んでいる友人から手紙が届く。

　みずえ様
　　昨夜は一晩で1メートル以上のドカ雪[1]が降りました。湿った重い雪で，今にも屋根が落ちてくるのではないかと心配です。雪がやんだら早速*雪かきをしなければなりません。でも私も年ですから，屋根の上に登っての雪かきはとてもつらいのです。こんな時3人の息子がそばにいてくれたらと思うのですが，雪かきのために東京や大阪から，息子たちを*呼び寄せるわけにもいきません。
　　ご近所の家も同じ悩みを抱えていて，困っているようです。毎年同じようなお便りばかりで申し訳ないと思いますが，ほかに書くことも思いつきません。
　　春になってお目にかかれるのを楽しみにしております。
　　　　　　　　　　　　　　　　　　　　　　　　　ひろ子

　友人の言うとおり，北陸地方を中心とした，北海道，東北，山陰の日本海沿岸は豪雪地帯である。*除雪が機械化されてだいぶ

32　II．日本の季節

6. Heavy Snow and Bougainvilleas

The Japanese archipelago stretches for 3,000 kilometers from north to south, so there are tremendous differences in climate.

In February, I received the following letter from my friend in Toyama Prefecture.

Dear Mizue,

Last night it snowed all through the night with more than one meter falling in one huge downpour. It is wet, heavy snow, and we are still worried that the roof may fall in. After the snow stops, we must immediately start shovelling off the snow. But I am old, and it is very hard to get up on the roof to take off the snow. I wish my three sons could come and help with this work, but, of course, I cannot call them here from Tokyo and Osaka.

The other houses in the neighborhood all have the same problem, and we are really in a pickle. I seem to write the same thing to you every year around this time. But there is certainly no other news as important as this.

I am looking forward to meeting you in the spring.

All the best,
Hiroko

Hokkaido, and the northern regions of Tohoku and San-in along the coast of the Sea of Japan, centering around Hoku-

楽になったらしいが、屋根の*雪おろしは個々の家でするしかない。手伝いに行ってあげたいが、こちらにも仕事があってそうもいかない。深刻な問題である。

　同じころ、沖縄にいる教え子から手紙が届く。

佐々木先生

　先生、お元気でいらっしゃいますか？　こちらに来て一年になりますが、コートのいらない沖縄の冬を楽しんでいます。東京は今ごろ*からっ風が吹いて*底冷えのする日が続いているのでしょうね。こちらはもう春です。島のあちこちにブーゲンビリアとかいろいろの花が咲き乱れ、海から運ばれてくる潮風にも春の香りがします。

　お忙しいとは思いますが、*思い切って一週間くらい休暇をとってこちらにいらっしゃいませんか。今は観光客も少ないし、沖縄にいらっしゃるには一番よいころだと思います。

　こちらにいらっしゃるのを心待ちにしております。

　　　　　　　　　　　　　　　　　　　　　　かしこ

　日本に住みながら同時に受け取った2通の手紙のなんと違うこ

34　Ⅱ．日本の季節

riku where my friend lives, form the heavy snowfall region of the country. They now have heavy snow ploughs and other machines to help with the snow moving work, so it is probably much easier now. But getting the snow off the roofs still has to be done by the individual families in each house. We would like to go and help, of course, but we have to work here, so we can't. It is a serious problem.

At about the same time a letter arrived from one of my former students living in Okinawa.

Dear Mrs. Sasaki,

I hope you are well. It is one year since I came here. The Okinawa winter is so mild you do not need a coat. I enjoy it very much. In Tokyo now I expect there are dry winds blowing and chilly days will continue for a while yet. It is already spring here. All over the island bougainvilleas and other flowers are blooming in profusion, swept by the warm breezes coming in off the ocean.

I am sure you are very busy, but wouldn't it be possible for you to arrange to take off a week and come here for a holiday? There are not many tourists here now. It's the best time to come to Okinawa.

I'm really looking forward to welcoming you here.

Regards,

Isn't it remarkable what a difference there is between these

と。自分で行くより富山の友人を沖縄に行かせてあげたいものだ。どんなに喜ぶだろうか。

VOCABULARY   *Yukikaki:* shovelling snow   *Yobiyoseru:* call   *Josetsu:* snow moving   *Yukioroshi:* getting down the snow   *Karakkaze:* dry wind   *Sokobie:* chilly   *Omoikitte~suru:* arrange to

注────────────────
1. ドカ雪
   一度に大量に降る雪。

letters I received at the same time from two people living in Japan? I would love to send my friend from Toyama to Okinawa, rather than go myself. It would do her good and I am sure she would be very pleased about that.

NOTES

1. Heavy snow: It snows a lot at the same time.

Ⅲ. 年中行事

1. お正月

　元たんの朝早く，神社や寺院にお参りをして，開運札をいただき，一年の幸運を祈る習慣を初もうでといいます。東京なら明治神宮，名古屋なら熱田神宮というように，人の集まる神社は決まっています。この日ばかりはほとんどの鉄道は終夜運転で，12月31日の夜更けから，明治神宮などは，晴れ着を着た人たちでごったがえします。

　一年の初まりは初もうでからという人も多いでしょう。

　日本人にとって新年，お正月はあらゆるものが新しく始まるということでもあります。

　伝統的な飾りものの*門松は家の入口におかれます。門松は*常緑樹である松と生命力の強い竹でできていて，健康で長生きできるようにという願いをあらわしています。

　お正月の間はほとんどの店は閉まっています。人々はおせち料理を*重箱に用意して，よくそれを食べます。おせち料理は長持ちするので，お母さんや奥さんたちはふだんのわずらわしい家事から解放されます。

　しかし，日本人にとってのお正月も年々変わってきています。年中開いているスーパーマーケットはあるし，またおせち料理は

III. Annual Events and Seasonal Phenomena

1. O-Shogatsu

Early on New Year's day there is the custom of Hatsu-mode, the First Shrine Visit of the Year, when people go to a Shinto shrine to receive a good luck amulet and pray for good fortune during the coming year. The shrines where people gather are generally the same. For example in Tokyo it is Meiji Jingu. In Nagoya it is Atsuta Jingu. It is only on this day that most railways operate all night and, on midnight of December 31, shrines like Meiji Jingu are crowded with people dressed in their best clothes.

There are many people who say that the New Year begins with one's first shrine visit.

For the Japanese, the New Year, O-Shogatsu, represents the time when everything starts afresh.

Kadomatsu, a traditional decoration, are placed at the entrances to people's homes. They are made of pine, for being evergreen, and bamboo which has a very long life. Kadomatsu, therefore, represent the wish for health and longevity.

Over the New Year period, the majority of shops are closed.

口に合わないということから、おせち料理を食べない家庭も増えています。日本の伝統的な習慣が少しずつ失われていくのは残念なことです。

VOCABULARY　*Kadomatsu:* New Year's pine decoration
Joryokuju: evergreen tree　*Jubako:* a nest of lacquered boxes

2.　成人の日

　日本では満20歳になると大人として認められます。参政権が与えられ、飲酒なども公式に許されます。1月15日は「成人の日」で国民の祝日です。各市町村では成人を迎えた男女のために成人式が行われます。

3.　節　分

　2月3日の夜は「鬼は外、福は内」と言いながら豆をまきます。なぜ豆が使われるのかは明らかではありません。悪い事を追い払い、幸運を招くという儀式で、立春の前夜に行われます。

People eat O-sechi-ryori, special food that is served in sets of five-drawed lacquer boxes. As this food keeps well, mothers and wives are released from their normal household duties.

The Japanese O-Shogatsu, however, is changing year by year. Supermarkets now remain open and the number of families that do not eat O-sechi-ryori, on account of what they think is its poor taste, is increasing. Japanese traditional customs are slowly disappearing and it is very regrettable.

2. Adults Day (Coming-of-Age Day)

In Japan people officially become adults at the age of twenty and are permitted to drink alcohol and to vote. January 15 is Adults Day and a national holiday. At this time, ceremonies are held throughout the country for young men and women reaching 20 that year.

3. The Eve of Spring (The End of Winter)

On the evening of February 3, people throw handfuls of beans shouting "Devils out, Fortune in". Why beans are used is not clear. This takes place on the eve of the first day of spring as a ritual to drive evil out and to invite good fortune in.

4. ひな祭り

3月3日。ひな祭りは女の子の健康な成長を願うというものです。

赤いひな段の最上段には内裏様(だいり)、次の段には三人官女、三段目には五人ばやし、四段目は左大臣、右大臣と飾られます。近ごろは七、八段もあるものが売り出されていますが、狭い日本の家では、これを飾れる家がどれくらいあるでしょうか。

5. 入学式

春は物事が新しく始まる時です。枯れたように見える木々からは、柔らかい緑の芽が顔を出し、やがて花が咲きます。日本では学校も会社も4月に始まります。入学式、入園式、入社式はたいてい満開の桜の時季に行われます。日本人にとって、ものごとはこのように始まるのが自然なのです。

4. Hina Matsuri Dolls Festival

March 3. This is a festival to wish for the health and growth of little girls.

Dolls are arranged on a red, tiered stand with the Emperor and Empress on the top level. On the second level are three court ladies; on the third, five musicians and, on the fourth, the Minister of the Left and the Minister of the Right. Nowadays, stands with seven or eight levels are on sale but, since Japanese houses are generally lacking in space, the number of homes possessing them may be small.

5. Entrance Ceremonies

Spring is the time when everything starts fresh. Trees that seem to have withered and died display soft, green buds which then burst into blossom. In Japan, therefore, the school and business year begins in April. Almost all entrance ceremonies at schools and companies for new students and new employees take place when the cherry blossoms are in full bloom. For the Japanese, it is natural that this should be so.

6. 子供の日・端午の節句

5月5日。この日は武者人形を飾り，こいのぼりを立て，ちまきやかしわもちを食べて祝います。

5月は初夏の季節です。花の大部分が咲き乱れ，野山は新緑に包まれます。青空の下ではこいのぼりが泳ぎ，実に気持ちのよい季節です。

7. 七夕

天の川（銀河）の東西にある牽牛星（けんぎゅう）と織女星（しょくじょ）が年に1度だけ，7月7日の夜にであうという中国の伝説と日本古来の風習とが重なったものです。聖武天皇の天平6年（734年）から行われたといわれています。七夕竹に歌や願いごとを書いた色紙を結びつけます。

旧暦の7月はすでに秋で，秋の夜の天の川はとても美しいのに，それを新暦の7月に行うので，天の川が見えないこともよくあります。このごろでは七夕本来の意味から離れて，観光や商業中心になっていくのは残念なことです。

6. Children's Day, Boys' Festival

May 5. This is celebrated by putting a doll of a warrior on display and by hoisting carp streamers on a pole. Rice dumplings wrapped in bamboo leaves and oak leaves are eaten.

May is the beginning of summer when more flowers bloom than at any other time of the year and the mountains and meadows are covered afresh in green. With the carp streamers fluttering under blue skies this is indeed a pleasant season.

7. Tanabata, The Festival of the Weaver Star

This is a combination of a Chinese legend and an ancient Japanese custom according to which the two stars Altair (The Cowherd) and Vega (The Weaver Maiden), normally on opposite sides of the Milky Way, come together once a year on July 7. This festival is said to have begun under the Emperor Shomu in 734. Prayers and requests are written on pieces of coloured paper which are then tied to bamboo.

According to the old, lunar calendar, July was already autumn when the Milky Way in the night sky was especially beautiful. As the festival is now held according to the Gregorian calendar, it is often impossible to see the Milky Way at all. These days, therefore, it is regrettable that the festival has

8. 七五三

　11月15日に3歳，5歳の男児，3歳，7歳の女児を神社に参拝させる風習です。これは江戸の中期から始まったといわれています。11月15日の前後は各地の神社で，着飾った子供たちの姿を見ることができます。

9. 大みそか

　12月31日の夜のことです。年越しそばを，寺院がつく108の除夜の鐘を聞きながら食べます。幸せがそばのように長く続くようにという願いがこめられています。
　さあ，年越しそばを食べたら初もうでに行きましょう。そんなに寒がっていないで。

departed from its original purpose to become a tourist and commercial phenomenon.

8. Shichi-Go-San

On November 15 there is the custom of taking boys of three and five years of age, and girls of three and seven, to worship at Shinto shrines. It is said to have started in the middle of the Edo Period. On and around this day, children can be seen dressed in kimono at Shinto shrines everywhere.

9. O-Misoka

This refers to New Year's Eve. Toshikoshi Soba (noodles to see out the old year and see in the new) are eaten while listening to the sound of the one hundred and eight strokes of the Joya no Kane (Watching Bell) struck everywhere at Buddhist temples. It is hoped that happiness, like the soba noodles, will last for a long time.

When we've eaten our Toshikoshi Soba, lets go to a shrine for Hatsu-mode and not complain too much of the cold.

Ⅳ. 日本人の社会と生活

1. タテ社会

　日本の社会は，世界でも*特異なものとよくいわれる。それはなぜであろうか。

　日本は*地続きの*国境線がなく，*異質文化をもつ*異民族によって支配を受けたことがない。国籍，人種，宗教，言語，生活様式などが似かよった社会を形成している。

　この社会は細かなタテ関係によって分けられる。同じ実力を持つ会社員でも，年齢，入社年次，*勤続期間が長いか短いかなどによって*序列ができてくる。だから日本人は，自分が序列のどの位置にいるかを常に意識して行動している。ことばに尊敬語や謙譲語が存在するのもそのためだし，結婚式の席順やスピーチの*発言順までが，常に序列を意識して行われている。

　このタテ社会が日本の集団主義を*支えているといえるだろう。

VOCABULARY　　*Tokui:* singular, peculiar, unique, different　*Jitsuzuki:* land contiguity　　*Kokkyosen:* national boundary, border　*Ishitsubunka:* foreign, alien culture　　*Iminzoku:* different race, people　*Kinzoku kikan:* period of continuous, uninterrupted service　*Joretsu:* rank, grade, order　　*Hatsugenjun:* order of speaking, speeches　　***Sasaeru:*** support

IV.   Japanese Society and the Life of the People

1.   The Vertical Society

Why is it that, even by the rest of the world, Japanese society is often described as different or unique?

Japan has no national boundaries contiguous with other countries and has never come under the domination of a different race with a different culture. It constitutes a society based on similarity of nationality, race, religion, language and way of life.

This society is separated into fine vertical relationships. For example, although they may be of similar ability, company employees can be ranked according to age, year of entry into the organisation and length of continuous service, etc. It is for this reason that the behaviour of the Japanese is based on a constant awareness of what their position is in this hierarchy. Polite and humble forms of speech exist in the language for this purpose and even when it comes to the seating arrangement at a wedding, and the order of speeches, everything is always done according to rank.

It is this vertical society that supports and maintains the

2. 恥の文化

　日本人は集団になると，考えられないほど強い力を*発揮するが，個人個人の力はたいしたことはない，とよくいわれる。

　日本人は*仲間外れにされることを恐れる。だから強く自分を主張することよりも，周囲と*同調して，たとえ意見が違ったとしても「丸くおさめる」ことを好む。つまり自分自身の考えをもって*目立つことよりも，人の考えに同調して「*平均化」しようとする。

　こういう背景の中で，日本人は自分の行動に対する他人の批評に常に*気を配っている。他人にばかにされたり，何かを拒否されること，特にそれが*人前で行われた場合，*恥として感じる。

　ベネディクトは『菊と刀』[1]の中で「日本人は*恥辱感を*原動力にしている」と述べているが，確かにそのとおりだと思う。

　いくら社会が近代化したとしても，「恥」を原動力とする日本人の意識は，当分変わらないだろう。

VOCABULARY　　*Hakki suru:* display, demonstrate, exhibit　*Nakamahazure:* treat as an outsider, reject　　*Docho suru:* align, agree with others　　*Medatsu:* stand out, be conspicuous　　*Heikinka:* standardisation　　*Ki o kubaru:* be on the alert　　*Hitomae:* in front of others　　*Haji:* shame, disgrace, humiliation　　*Chijokukan:* sense of shame　　*Gendoryoku:* driving, motive force

group ideology of the Japanese people.

2. Culture of Shame

It is often said that, when the Japanese group together, they demonstrate unimaginable strength but that individually their strength is quite insignificant.

The Japanese fear rejection by the group. Therefore, rather than assert themselves powerfully as individuals, they prefer to align themselves with those around them even when their private opinions may differ. In other words, rather than stand out by virtue of their own ideas, they prefer to achieve standardisation by conforming to the ideas of others.

Against this background the Japanese are always on the alert for criticism of their actions from other people. To be made a fool of or to be rejected for some reason, especially in front of others, is a source of shame for the Japanese.

In her book, *The Chrysanthemum and the Sword*, Ruth Benedict states that the Japanese have made a sense of shame a driving force. I think that is exactly right.

No matter how much society is changed, with shame as their driving force, the sensibilities of the Japanese will remain unaltered for a long while to come.

注―――
1. 『菊と刀』　Ruth Fulton Benedict (1887—1948) 著。アメリカの文化人類学者。その日本文化研究『菊と刀』をとおして，日本でも学問上の影響が大きい。

3. 中流意識

日本人のほとんどは，自分が中流階級に属すると思っているし，実際にも，現代の日本では大多数の人が上もなければ下もない*均質な状況にある。

1980年の「社会*階層と社会移動」全国調査によると，威信，学歴，所得，財産，生活様式，権力という6つについて，すべてに高い人は1割，低い人は3割で，残りの6割の人は高かったり低かったりで，このへんが日本人が中流意識を持つ*根拠ではないだろうか。

*総理府が行っている「国民生活に関する意識調査」でも，自分が「中」であると答える人はこの15年ほど（高度成長のあと）一貫して90％前後になる。

しかし，これは自分は世間なみの生活をしている，だから自分は中流である，と思い込む*幻想にすぎないのではないだろうか。今，日本は高度成長から，*低成長の時代に入り，社会保障の内容は後退を続けている。

まさかの時に日本人は今までどおりの生活水準を*維持できるだけの資産を持っているだろうか。その時にも90％の人が自分を中流と答えるかどうかは疑わしい。

NOTES

1. *Kiku to Katana*: By Ruth Fulton Benedict (1887–1948). American cultural anthropologist who has had a great influence on scholarship in Japan through her book, *The Chrysanthemum and the Sword, Patterns of Japanese Culture* (1946).

3. Middle Class Consciousness

Almost all Japanese think of themselves as belonging to the middle class, and it is indeed a fact that, in contemporary Japan, the condition of the circumstances of the majority of the people are of considerable homogeneity.

According to the national "Social Strata and Social Movement" survey of 1980, based on the six categories: prestige, educational background, income, property, life style and power and influence, 10% of the population rate themselves "high" in every category and 30% as "low". The remaining 60% rate themselves as a mixture of high and low, and it is surely this latter which provides the foundation for the middle class consciousness of the Japanese people.

Similarly, according to the "Citizens' Life Awareness" survey carried out by the Prime Minister's Office, about 90% of those polled during the last fifteen years (i.e. after the period of high economic growth) regard themselves as "in the middle".

But perhaps this conviction that people who lead ordinary

VOCABULARY　　*Kinshitsu:* homogeneity　　*Kaiso:* social strata, class　　*Konkyo:* basis, foundation　　*Sorifu:* Prime Minister's Office　　*Genso:* illusion, fantasy　　*Teiseicho:* low growth rate　　*Iji suru:* maintain

4. 年功序列

　日本では一度会社に*就職したら，定年退職¹になるまで，その会社で働くのが普通である。アメリカのように，少しでも*待遇のよい職場を求めて変わる*風潮は日本にはないし，またそんなことをする人がいると「腰が軽い」などと陰口をたたかれる。

　日本の公共部門や大企業では，「年功序列」といって，*勤続年数や年齢が増すに従って地位が上がっていく体系をとるところが多い。当然のことながら，地位が上がるに従って，給料も増えていく。

　この制度ができたのは明治末期から昭和の初めといわれているが，社会の急激な変化で，この制度も大きな*矛盾を生み出している。たとえばバリバリ仕事をする20代の社員より，古い知識の持ち合わせしかなく，会社内で暇な時間をもてあましている50代の社員が，高額の給料を手にするというように。

lives are, by definition, middle class is an illusion. Afterall Japan has moved from a high period into a low period of economic growth, and there is a continuing decline in the substance of social security.

In case of an emergency, would the Japanese be able to maintain the standard of living and property-owning to which they have been accustomed? At such a time it is doubtful whether 90% of the Japanese would still reply that they are middle class.

4. Seniority Rule

In Japan, after employment has been found in a particular company or firm, it is usual to work there until the mandatory retirement age. Unlike America, the tendency to change jobs in search of even slightly better working conditions does not exist in Japan. Should anyone do so, that person is likely to be criticised behind his back for being "fickle".

In the public sector in Japan and the major corporations, promotion takes place according to the years of continuous service and age. It goes without saying that an increase in salary accompanies any rise in position.

This system is said to have developed between the end of the Meiji and the beginning of the Showa Period (1907–1930) but, in view of the sudden changes in Japanese society, it is one

最近では職務の*遂行能力によって，企業内での賃金格差を決定しようとする企業が出てきている。職業上の能力，勤務態度，*業績などが正当に評価され，地位や給料が決定されるとなれば，「肩たたき」²などという現象も姿を消すはずである。

VOCABULARY　　*Shushoku suru:* find employment　　*Taigu:* conditions　　*Fucho:* tendency　　*Kinzoku nensu:* number of years of continuous service　　*Mujun:* inconsistency, contradiction　　*Suiko:* performance, execution (of one's job)　　*Gyoseki:* results, achievements

注
1. 定年退職
   1983年の調査で定年制をとっている企業は全体の82％。その約半分が60歳定年制である。
2. 肩たたき
   会社・官庁などで高年齢者に退職をそれとなく勧めること。最近では「40歳肩たたき」などとさえ言われる。

5. 学歴偏重社会

　あなたは「教育ママ」ということばを聞いたことがありますか？　これは子供の教育に熱心すぎる母親たちを*皮肉ったことばなのです。しかし*一方的に母親たちを*責めてもよいのでしょうか。ここで彼女たちの話にも耳を傾けてみましょう。
　「主人は仕事で忙しいものですから，子供の教育は私に任され

that contains a number of important contradictions. For example, an employee in his fifties with out-of-date skills who hardly knows what to do with his spare time, will receive a far higher salary than a man in his twenties who performs his work with speed and energy.

Recently, however, there are companies attempting to decide wages on the basis of performance ability. If extra skills, attitude to work and results are properly assessed and position and salaries decided accordingly, the phenomenon known as, Kata-tataki, "the tap on the shoulder", should disappear.

NOTES

1. Mandatory Retirement Age: According to a survey carried out in 1983, 82% of companies and businesses have a retirement policy and, of these, half set the age at sixty years.
2. *Kata-tataki*: "The Tap on the shoulder" refers to the method of recommending indirectly to elderly employees in companys and government offices that they should retire. Recently it is said to take place even at the age of forty.

5. The Over-emphasis on Educational Background

Have you ever heard of the expression "Education Mama"? It is sarcastically applied to Japanese mothers who are over zealous with regard to the education of their children. But is it right to criticise such mothers in this one-sided way? Here is what one such mother has to say.

っぱなしです。うちの息子はまだ小学生ですから、学校から帰ってきたら遊ばせたいと思うのはどの親も同じだと思うのです。でも現実には、息子の友人は皆*塾に行っているし、うちの息子だけ勉強に遅れれば、結局社会にとり残されてしまいます。そうなれば息子もかわいそうです。よい高校[1]に入り、よい大学を出て、よい会社に就職し、よい仕事を得る。何も私だけがこう考えているわけではありません。日本の社会の*仕組みがこうなっているんですもの、仕方ないですわ。結局は息子の幸福のためなのです。」

彼女の*弁解はあまりにも当然で*非難する気もおこらなくなります。この風潮はいったいいつまで続くのでしょうか。「学歴偏重社会」が続く限り、教育ママはますます増えていく気がします。中には3歳から塾に通わせる母親もいるそうです。よい幼稚園に入ることで、そのままエスカレーター式に中学、高校、大学と行けるからです。

「学生時代を受験勉強して過ごさせるのはかわいそうですから。本を読んだり、スポーツをしたり、充実した学生生活を過ごさせるには、この方法しかないのです」とエスカレーター式の学校（主に有名私立校）に息子や娘を入れている母親たちは言います。しかし、こういう学校は授業料なども年間100万円くらいと大変高く、ごく一部の人たちしかそうすることはできないでしょう。

教育とはいったいなんでしょうか。小さな頭にたくさんのことを暗記させることでしょうか。これからの社会に必要なのは、自分で考え行動できる人間ではないでしょうか。

"My husband is busy with his job so he leaves the question of the children's education entirely up to me. My son is at elementary school. I'm like any other mother, I think, in wanting to let him go out and play when he comes home but, as his friends are attending privately run cramming schools, he has to do as well. This is because I do not want to see him left behind in his school work and then, as a result, left behind by society. If things turn out like that it will be miserable for him. I want him to go to a good school and a good university and get a good job in a good company. It's not just me who thinks like this. This is the way Japanese society is organised. So you've got to accept it. It's for my son's own good that I make him study the way he does".

This mother's explanation is so reasonable, one does not feel like trying to criticise it at all. But how much further will such tendencies in education go? As long as this overemphasis on education and educational background persists in Japan, the phenomenon of the "Education Mama" will increase even more. Some such mothers even send their children to private cramming schools when they are only three years old. This is so that they can enter prestigious kindergartens and, from there, proceed, escalator-fashion, to obtain easy entrance to the middle schools and high schools with which such kindergartens are connected, and then on to a prestigious university.

Mothers who enter their sons and daughters into these "escalator-style" schools (mainly famous private schools) ex-

VOCABULARY　　*Hinikuru:* speak sarcastically of　　*Ippoteki:* one-sided　　*Semeru:* attack, criticise　　*Juku:* privately run coaching or cramming schools　　*Shikumi:* structure, contrivance　　*Benkai:* explanation, justification　　*Hinan:* criticism, blame

注
1. 高校進学率
　義務教育は小学校6年，中学校3年だが，日本の高校進学率は94.1% (1985) と非常に高い。

6. 単身赴任

　昔なら，親が*転勤することになったら，子供も*転校したものだ。「親の仕事の都合で，小学校，中学校と3回も転校しました」と聞いてもだれも不思議に思わなかった。
　しかし近ごろでは，子供の教育のため，家族を残したまま転勤するサラリーマンが多い。慣れない土地で勤務し，仕事から帰っても家にはだれもいない。待っているのは暗い部屋。料理，洗濯と慣れない作業も加わる。

cuse themselves, "it's pitiful to see children spend their school days doing nothing but preparing for entrance exams. I want them to enjoy themselves at school reading books for pleasure and enjoying sports and games. This is the only way to let them do so". But the annual fees of about ¥1,000,000 at such schools are extremely high and few people can afford them.

What is education? Is it just a question of drumming facts into the heads of small children? What society needs from now on is people who have been trained to think for themselves.

NOTES
1. Compulsory education in Japan consists of six years' elementary school and three at middle school but the rate of students who go on to high schools is very high (94.1% in 1985).

6. Single Posting

It used to be the case that, when a man was transferred to a new post in a different part of the country, his family would go with him, his children transferring to a new school. No one thought it strange to hear someone say "as a child I had to change elementary and middle school three times on account of my father's job".

Recently, however, there are many company employees who,

7割以上の会社が，単身赴任者に月額2～3万円の*別居手当て，3割の会社が月1～2回の*帰宅手当てを*支給しているという。

　だが，決して金銭で解決できる問題ではない。月に数回しか会わない夫婦，父親の顔も見ずに育つ子供たち，日本の家庭生活の*崩壊の一因がこんなところにもある。

　最近，単身赴任の家庭に起こる物質的・精神的な問題が*社会問題化してきた。単身赴任保険[1]などという変わった保険もできた。

　大きな社会問題となる前に，家族が一緒に暮らせる方法が考えられるべきだろう。

VOCABULARY　　*Tenkin:* tranfer to a new post　　*Tenko:* transfer to a new school　　*Bekkyoteate:* "separate living" (separation) allowance　　*Kitakuteate:* allowance (permitting one) to return home　　***Shikyu suru:*** provide, supply　　*Hokai:* breakdown　　***Shakai mondaika:*** become a social problem

because of their children's education, leave their families behind when they are transferred to new jobs. This means that, working in an unfamiliar place, they have no one to come home to when the day's work is over. A dark room is all that is waiting for them. And there are also the additional unfamiliar chores like doing their own cooking and laundry.

Seventy percent of all companies and firms give an extra "separation allowance" of ¥20,000–¥30,000 above their normal salaries to employees who have been transferred to a single posting. Thirty percent of companies also provide such people with an extra allowance to enable them to return to their homes once or twice a month.

But this is definitely not a problem that can be solved with money. When married couples are able to meet only a few times a month and children are growing up without seeing their father's face, it is little wonder that family life in Japan is on the point of breakdown.

Recently, the various material and psychological difficulties arising in homes affected by the single posting phenomenon have escalated into something of a social problem. There is even a curious Single Posting Insurance Policy which has come into existence.

Before a major social problem arises, a means whereby families can live together has to be found.

注

1. 単身赴任保険
   その内容　①日本国内で単身者が傷害事故に遭った場合，家族が看護にかけつける交通費や宿泊費などを補償する。②留守家族が傷害事故で7日以上入院した時は，単身者の帰省費用を負担する，など。

7. 勤務時間と休暇

「*勤勉」ということばは日本人の代名詞になった。子供の時はよく学び，大人になると「ハチ」のようによく働く。「働くことは*美徳である」という*倫理感と労働時間の長さ（表参照）が勤勉な日本人を作りあげているともいえる。

先進国の年間総労働時間　（1983年労働省推計）

西ドイツ	1613時間	イギリス	1938時間
フランス	1657時間	日　　本	2152時間
アメリカ	1898時間		

上の表からもはっきり分かるように，ヨーロッパの中でも経済力の強い西ドイツが1613時間なのに比較し，日本人は1年に539時間（1日8時間労働として67日）も多く働いていることになる。

「日本の経済は，働きバチ日本人に支えられている」と*皮肉を言われても仕方がない。

NOTES

1. Single Posting Insurance Policy: Amongst other things this guarantees that (1) in the case of a man on a single posting incurring accident or injury, the travelling and accommodation expenses will be paid for his family to go and take care of him and that (2) in the case of a member of the family of a man on a single posting being hospitalised for more than seven days, the cost of the expenses incurred during his return home will be paid.

7. Work and Leisure

"Industrious" has become a synonym for the Japanese people. They study hard at school and go on, as adults, to be as busy as worker bees. It can also be said, however, that the phenomenon of the industrious Japanese has been brought about by the morality, according to which "work is a virtue" as well as long working hours (see chart).

Total Annual Working Hours in Advanced Countries

W. Germany	1613	England	1938
France	1657	Japan	2152
America	1898		

As can be clearly seen, compared with the 1613 hours of W. Germany, the strongest economic power in Europe, the Japanese work 539 hours more (i.e. 67 extra eight-hour days). Confronted with such statistics it is difficult to object to the

「遊び」についていえばいま一番よく遊んでいるのは大学生だろう。なにしろそれまでは受験勉強に追われて遊ぶのを*我慢してきたし，大学を出たあとは「働きバチ」の一生が待っているのだから。

ビジネスマンの遊びといえばマージャンかゴルフなど，しかしこれも仕事上の*義務であることが多い。

ここまで成長した日本経済にとって，これほどの労働時間は本当に必要だろうか。日本人にとって「遊びの*哲学」が*確立されてもよい時期にきている気がする。

VOCABULARY　*Kinben:* industrious, diligent, hard working
Bitoku: virtue　　*Rinrikan:* moral values, sense of values, ethics
Hiniku: sarcasm　　*Gaman suru:* endure, go without　　*Gimu:* duty
Tetsugaku: philosophy　　*Kakuritsu suru:* establish, found

8. 日本の宗教

正月は神社[1]に*初もうでに行くが，結婚式はキリスト教で挙げ，お*葬式は仏教でというように，日本には特有の宗教観が日常生活の中に溶け込んでいる。

神道は日本でもっとも古い宗教であり，*自然崇拝に始まり祖先崇拝を本流とする。このため神道には多くの神々が登場する。

仏教は紀元前5世紀ごろインドで始まり，日本に伝えられたのは6世紀とされている。*伝来宗教である仏教は日本人の生活に大きな影響を与えているが，日本*古来の*民族信仰である神道も

sarcastic remark that "the Japanese economy is supported by the worker bees".

As for "enjoyment", it is the university students who are enjoying themselves the most. But that is hardly surprising as they had to endure a life empty of enjoyment in order to pass their university entrance examinations. And, once they have graduated, it is the life of the worker bee that awaits them.

Enjoyment for the company employee means mahjong and golf etc. but, in many cases, these become extra duties they must perform over and above their normal work.

In view of the degree of Japanese economic growth, are such long working hours really necessary? The time is ripe for the establishment of a "philosophy of leisure" for the Japanese people.

8. Japanese Religion

Everyday life in Japan is infused with an unusual religious sensibility. At the New Year, people go to Shinto shrines for Hatsu-mode but weddings may be performed according to Christian ceremony and funerals according to Buddhist ritual.

Shinto is the old religion of Japan. It is said to have begun in nature worship, then developed mainly into ancestor worship and, for that reason, it contains many gods.

Buddhism evolved in India in the fifth century B.C. and is

存続している。このように長期間にわたって2つの宗教が*両立しているところに日本の宗教の特徴がある。

日本のキリスト教はまだ歴史も浅く、クリスチャンの総数も国民の約1％にすぎない。

日本人の宗教観はだんだん薄れているといわれるが、それでも、神棚² と仏壇³ を供える家庭はまだ多くみうけられる。また形に表れない場合でも、日本人の精神の奥深くに、仏教、神道に*根ざした宗教観が*宿っているといえる。

VOCABULARY　*Hatsu-mode:* the first visit of the New Year to a Shinto Shrine (See p. 38)　*Soshiki:* funeral　*Shizen suhai:* nature worship　*Denrai shukyo:* imported religion　*Korai:* ancient, from time immemorial　*Minzoku shinko:* popular religious belief　*Ryoritsu suru:* coexist, exist together　*Nezasu:* be rooted in　*Yadoru:* dwell in

注────────────────────────
1. 神社
   日本人固有の信仰対象となった神がまつってある。現在日本に約8万社ある。
2. 神棚
   家の中に神社からもらった御札などがまつってある棚。
3. 仏壇
   仏像や位はい（死者の戒名を書いた木の札）を安置してある壇。

reckoned to have reached Japan in the sixth century A.D. As an imported religion, Buddhism exerts a great influence on the lives of the Japanese people, but Shinto, the native religious belief, continues to endure. That two religions have existed together in this way since ancient times is a particular feature of the spiritual life of the Japanese people.

Christianity has only a brief history in Japan and the number of believers is only about 1% of the population.

It is said that the religious sense of the Japanese is becoming weaker but, despite that, there are still many homes that can be seen with Shinto or Buddhist altars. Furthermore, there are many unspecified ways in which a religious sense, rooted in Buddhism and Shinto, continues to dwell in the recesses of the Japanese spirit.

NOTES

1. Shinto shrine: A place dedicated to a religious object native to the Japanese which is worshipped as a god. In Japan, today, there are about 80,000 Shinto shrines.
2. Shinto altar: A shelf upon which is displayed a religious amulet received from a Shinto shrine.
3. Buddhist altar: An altar upon which is displayed a statue of Buddha or memorial tablets inscribed with the posthumous names of deceased members of the family.

9. 男女雇用機会均等法

「男女雇用機会均等法」とは1986年4月から*実施された新しい法律だ。*法律用語は固苦しくて、分かりにくいけれど、とにかく読んでみよう。

目的
第1条 この法律は、法の下の*平等を 保障する 日本国憲法の理念にのっとり雇用の分野における 男女の均等な 機会及び*待遇が確保されることを促進するとともに……（後略）

一つの文章が非常に長いのでここで切ることにする。法の下の平等は、*憲法ができた時から 保障されていた。しかし男女を平等に雇う企業がどれだけあっただろう。女子は大学を出ても入社試験を受ける機会さえ与えられず、高い能力をもった人が、つまらない仕事に*甘んじてきたのだ。少なくともこの法律ができたおかげで、女子が新しい職場に進出する可能性が生まれた。

*募集、*採用、*配置、*昇進については努力規定、一定の福利厚生、定年、退職、*解雇については 禁止規定 となっているが、罰則なしと加えてあるのがどうも気になる。守らなくても罰則はないということで、守らない*不心得な 会社も多いのではないだろうか。

「男は仕事、女は家庭」という*概念が日本の社会全体に広くいきわたっているため、法律ができたからといって、急に女性の部長や課長が多く出現するとは思えない。家庭をもった女性がフル

9. Equal Opportunities for Women

The Equal Employment Opportunity Law was passed by the Japanese Diet in April 1986. The text is full of legalistic terminology and very difficult to follow, but let's read some of it.

Purpose.
Clause 1. This law aims to promote and clearly establish equality of opportunity and treatment in those areas of employment for which the Japanese constitution guarantees equality before the law, and...

The sentence is very long, so we cut it off here. Equality before the law was promulgated in the Japanese constitution introduced after the war. But then, how many companies do you think were pursuing a policy of equality of opportunity for women and men? Most women university graduates are not even given the chance to take the examinations for entrance into the companies. Those who do it often have great ability but are given boring jobs to do. Now, because of this law at least it is possible that women will be able to enter new areas of work.

Recruiting, employment, placement, and promotion are now to be determined by *ability*, and the addition of a *clause prohibiting* fixed compound benefits, pension, retirement, and discharge is indeed remarkable. Since there is no penalty for

タイムで働いていると,「ご主人に 理解があってよいですね」などと言われる。 この言葉自体が 日本人の職業意識を*裏付けるものだろう。女性が男性と*肩を並べて 仕事をしていくためには,まず私たちの意識から変えていかなければならない。

　もっとも本当に男女が平等に働ける時が来たら,こんな法律は必要なくなると思うのだが……。

VOCABULARY　　*Jisshi sareta:* passed　　*Horitsu yogo:* legalistic terminology　　*Byodo:* equality　　*Taigu:* treatment　　*Kenpo:* constitution　　*Amanjiru:* have to put up with　　*Boshu:* recruiting　　*Saiyo:* employment　　*Haichi:* placement　　*Shoshin:* promotion　　*Kaiko:* discharge　　*Fukokoroe na:* delinquent　　*Gainen:* notion　　*Urazukeru:* support　　*Kata o narabete:* on an equal footing

10. 見合い結婚

　結婚とは男女の継続的共同生活——日本では江戸時代のころから「*見合い」が行われ,夫婦が誕生してきた。

　見合い,つまり第三者の*仲立ちによってお互いに一*面識もない男女が引き合わされる。お互いに気に入れば結婚へと進むし,運悪くお互いが気に入らないとき,あるいは気に入っても相手に気に入られなければ,その話はご破算になる。

　見合いは間に立つ人が, 両家の生活条件とか, 結婚条件をみた上で話を進めるので, あまり*不釣り合いな 組み合わせは生まれ

not abiding by the regulation, undoubtedly there will be many delinquent companies who will ignore it.

The notion that "the man goes to work, and the woman takes care of the family" is firmly established throughout Japanese society. Even though we now have this law it does not mean that there will be a sudden increase in the number of women in management positions in Japanese companies. A woman with a family working full time is often told that "You are lucky to have the support of your husband." These words themselves surely indicate the attitude of the Japanese. For women to be able to go out to work *on an equal footing* with men, first we have to change our consciousness.

If a time does come when men and women can work on an equal basis, I think this law will then be unnecessary.

10. Arranged Marriages (Miai Kekkon)

Marriage is the union of man and woman in continuing life together. In Japan, Miai began to take place in the Edo Period when the phenomenon of the married couple came into existence.

The miai, itself, is when a third person introduces to each other a man and a woman, who are perfect strangers, with a view to their getting married. If the two are attracted to each other they may go on to marry. If things do not go

ない。第三者が理性的に判断して紹介するのだから，結婚したあとも2人の間に，あまり食い違いがおこらず，*離婚率も低い。

　女子高校生300人に「見合い結婚か恋愛結婚か」アンケートをとったところ，70%が見合い結婚と答えたそうである。これは東京でのことだから，地方に行けばその割合はもっと高くなるだろう。やはり皆，熱烈な恋愛より安全な結婚生活の方が大事なのだろうか。

VOCABULARY　　*Miai:* meeting with a prospective husband or wife　　*Nakadachi:* intermediary, go-between　　*Menshiki:* acquaintance　　*Futsuriai:* unbalance, disproportion　　*Rikon ritsu:* divorce rate

11.　安全・確実な日本の社会

　「日本の社会で生活して，どんなことを感じましたか」こんな質問を日本に住む留学生たちにしてみました。その答えを少しまとめてみましょう。

　●郵便が速く確実に届くこと。

well and they take a dislike to each other; or if one likes the other but the feeling is not mutual, then the discussions are called off.

The person who acts as go-between only recommends a miai meeting after due consideration is given to the respective circumstances of the two families involved and their terms of marriage. For this reason, ill-matched couples are few. The go-between introduces couples on the basis of a reasoned decision so that, after marriage, mistakes are rare and the rate of divorce is low.

According to a survey of three hundred girls who were asked in a questionnaire "Which is preferable, arranged miai marriage or love marriage?", seventy percent answered "miai". As this survey took place in Tokyo, it can be assumed that this percentage would have been higher in the provinces. Does this mean that people think a stable married life is more important than love?

11. A Safe and Stable Society

I have asked many foreign students in Japan, "What are your feelings about living in Japan?" The following is a brief summary of typical answers.

■ The mail is fast and reliable.

- 公衆電話が便利なこと，壊れている電話があまりないこと。
- どんな小さな食堂でも清潔で安心して食べられること。
- 道路が整備されていること，電車もバスも時刻表どおりに動き，ほとんど遅れないこと。
- 夜も安全で，どこでも１人で歩けること。
- 労働者がよく働き，建築・道路工事もすぐ終わること。

　その他にもまだたくさんの意見がありましたが，どの留学生も日本の社会を信頼できると感じていることはうれしいことです。
　これは日本の産業基盤（港湾施設や道路など）がしっかりしていることで，安全確実に仕事が運ぶということもあるでしょう。物を買うにも，仕事をするにも，すべて信頼のうえに物事が成り立っています。
　「急速に経済成長し，しかも 信頼できる社会を作り出した秘密はなんですか？」
　こんな質問をされて答えられる日本人がいるでしょうか。日本人にとって，電車が時間どおりに着いたり，どこにでも壊れていない公衆電話があるのは，当たり前のことなのですから。

- Public telephones are very useful and they never seem to be out of order.
- No matter how small the restaurant, it is always clean and the food safe to eat.
- The roads are very well maintained. The trains and buses usually run on schedule, and are very rarely late.
- It is safe to walk about alone after dark.
- The Japanese are hard working and conscientious. Especially in construction: buildings and roadworks are soon completed.

There are plenty of other opinions, but it is certainly comforting to know that foreign students feel that Japanese society is safe and its services are reliable.

The reliable industrial base of Japan (such as harbor facilities and roads) is certainly a major factor contributing to this situation, since it provides a secure working environment. Whether selling goods or performing services, the tasks are accomplished efficiently and safely.

"What is the secret to build a reliable, secure society that can achieve high growth rates?"

I wonder if there really are Japanese who can respond effectively when asked this question. The fact is that we just take things like the trains arriving on schedule and telephones operating properly for granted, and it is hard to explain what you never have to consciously think about.

V. 日本の文化

1. 日本の音楽

　日本の音楽を大きく2つに分けるとすれば*邦楽と*洋楽になると思います。

　邦楽とは古代に*公家や殿上人の音楽であった*雅楽，中世に武士階級の音楽であった*能楽，そして江戸時代，庶民の音楽であった俗曲などを言います。こうみてくると，日本の音楽は*ずいぶん*階級的な色彩が濃いですね。もちろん現在では，この階級的な区別はなくなりつつありますが。

　明治になって，洋楽が日本に入ってきました。洋楽輸入時代というわけですね。20世紀の今，邦楽は洋楽や歌謡曲に勢力を奪われた感じがします。テレビやラジオからはいつも演歌[1]や和製ポップスが流れ，小学校や中学校でも邦楽を教えることはしません。

　しかし時代を超えて生き続けてきた雅楽，能楽，俗曲などが，そう簡単に消えてしまうはずはありません。ふだんはクラシック音楽に耳を傾ける人も，お正月ともなれば雅楽の調べに，日本の伝統音楽のよさを*しみじみと味わったりするのです。

　最近では琴でバッハのバロック音楽を演奏するなど，邦楽に西洋音楽の*手法を取り入れたり，逆に西洋音楽の作曲家たちが，

78　V. 日本の文化

V. Japanese Cultural Activities

1. Japanese Music

Music in Japan can be broadly classified into Japanese and Western music.

Classical Japanese music includes the music of the court nobility, known as gagaku (court music); the musical accompaniment to performances of the Noh drama, associated with the samurai class in the Middle Ages; and the ballad music of the common people in the Edo period. This list shows that Japanese music is intensely associated with social classes who supported its original development. Today, these class associations are gradually disappearing.

Western music arrived in Japan in the Meiji era, when a lot of music (along with other forms of culture) were imported. At the moment, Japanese classical music seems to have lost its influence to Western music and popular songs (enka). On television and radio most of what is broadcast is popular ballads and Japanese pop songs. Classical Japanese music is not taught in grade schools.

However, the ancient court music, the music of the Noh, and ballad music in general, have survived throughout the

日本の伝統音楽に*題材を求めたり，邦楽と洋楽の間の*垣根が取り払われたようです。21世紀の音楽は両方の長所を取り入れたすばらしいものになっていくでしょう。

音階

　日本の伝統音楽は5音*音階です。1オクターブを基準に考え，西洋音楽からみれば何か欠けているような気がしますが，世界の民族音楽の中には案外この音階が多いのです。トルコやハンガリーの音楽を聞いて，どこか日本の民謡に似ているような気がするのは，そのせいかもしれません。

リズム

　日本人はよく，リズム感が悪いとかリズム*音痴が多いとかいわれますが，日本のリズムは1拍の長さが同じでなく，伸びたり縮んだりするのです。それに西洋音楽のリズムの基本が強弱という要素にあるのに対して，日本の音楽では強弱はそれほど重要ではありません。これは英語やドイツ語が強弱のアクセントがあるのに対して，日本語は高低アクセントであるのとよく似ていますね。
　リズム音痴というのは，あくまでも西洋音楽を主にして考えた時のことばなのです。

ages and will not disappear that easily. People who usually listen to Western classical music will often turn to Japanese traditional music at such times as New Year and learn to appreciate its finer points.

There have been some very interesting developments recently in the interaction between Japanese and Western music. Baroque music, such as that of Bach, has been played on the koto; techniques used in Western music have been tried out in Japanese music; and the reverse has also occurred with Western composers using themes from traditional Japanese music in their works. The fences between Western and Japanese music are being removed in this way. Prospects for very beautiful music combining the strengths of both styles in the next century look very good.

Musical scale

There are five tones to the musical scale of traditional Japanese music. From the viewpoint of Western music with its base of one octave, one has the feeling that there is something missing in Japanese music. It is, however, a surprising fact that there are many examples of this scale among the folk music of the world. When we listen to the music of Turkey or Hungary, there seem to be remarkable similarities with the folk music of Japan, and this may be due to the similar scales.

Rhythm

Japanese people are often told that they have no feeling for

VOCABULARY   *Hogaku:* Japanese music   *Yogaku:* Western music   *Kuge:* courtiers   *Gagaku:* court music   *Nogaku:* noh music   *Zuibun:* very much   *Kaikyu:* class associations   *Shimizimi ajiwau:* learn to appreciate   *Shuho:* method   *Daizai:* themes   *Kakine:* fences   *Onkai:* musical scale   *Onchi:* no feeling for

注

1. 演歌

    日本人に好まれる歌謡曲の主流。形式は西洋音楽のスタイルに似ているが、歌詞の内容、リズム感は日本の音楽に近い。伴奏は洋楽器のピアノ、バイオリンなどを使う。

2. 能と狂言

能と狂言を*総称して「能楽」と呼びますが、こう呼ばれるようになったのは明治以後のことで、江戸時代までは「猿楽」と呼ばれていました。

奈良時代に中国の唐から手品や曲芸などを見せる「散楽」と呼ばれる大衆芸能が伝わりました。これが平安時代に*こっけいな

V. 日本の文化

rhythm, but Japanese music employs beats of varying lengths. Lengthening and shortening beats is an important feature in the overall musical effect. Thus, stress elements, which form the basis of rhythm in Western music, are not so important in Japanese music. This distinction is very similar to that between the different languages. English and German have a stress accent, but pronunciation in the Japanese language depends on a pitch accent.

Thus, the accusation of being deaf to rhythm only stands when one considers the situation from the standpoint of Western music.

NOTES

1. *Enka*: The mainstream popular folksongs which are extremely popular in Japan. Formally they resemble Western music in style, but the content of the lyrics and the rhythm is closer to traditional Japanese music. Western instruments are used such as pianos and violins.

2. Noh and Kyogen

Noh and kyo-gen are usually collectively referred to under the name of noh drama (Nohgaku), a term which has only been in use since the Meiji era. They were called sarugaku until the end of the Edo period.

During the Nara period public entertainment like juggling,

*物まねの演技を 見せるものに 変わっていきました。さ̇る̇は物ま
ねが得意ですから，この大衆芸能はさ̇ん̇が̇く̇からさ̇る̇が̇く̇になっ
たとも言われています。

　鎌倉時代になって，こっけいな物まね芸よりは，まじめな内容
をもったうたや舞いが多くなってきます。ここで能という音楽，
*舞踊劇と狂言という*対話劇へと分かれるのです。

　室町時代に観阿弥[1]，世阿弥[2] の親子が能を芸術的なものへと発
展させます。それ以後，江戸時代を通じて現在に至るまで，能と
狂言は一番ずつ交互に上演されます。まるで同じ母親から生まれ
た二卵性双生児のように，二つはまったく違っていながら，よく
似ているのです。

　能は屋根のある特別な舞台で 演じられます。役者は能面[3]（のうめん）をつ
け，*能装束（のうしょうぞく）を着ます。*仮面は変身のための一つの手段で，世界
の各地にも同様に仮面劇があります。

　出演者はシテ方[4]（たいてい面をつける）とワキ方[5]（面をつけな
い）とおはやし方（笛や太鼓の楽器を演奏する人）の人たちです。
またシテ，ワキ以外の役はすべてツレと呼ばれます。

　舞台には 舞台装置といったものはまったくありません。謡[6]（うたい）の
文句を聞いて，音楽や役者の動きから，観客である私たちが，大
きな山や地震を想像するのです。

　さあ，説明はこれくらいにして舞台を見ましょう。おはやしが
聞こえます。シテが 白い足袋だけで*すり足で歩いています。こ
れは能の動作でもっとも特徴があります。あの歩き方はむずかし
いのでしょうか。能面をつけていて表情が見えません。

　能が終わり，舞台が狂言に変わると，張り詰めていた私たちの
気持ちも一気にほぐれます。舞台では，酒好きの主人公が酔う場

84　V. 日本の文化

conjuring and acrobatics, collectively called sangaku, was brought to Japan from the China of the Tang dynasty. This developed into humorous mimicry in the Heian period. It is said that these public entertainments came to be called sarugaku, replacing the term sangaku, because monkeys (saru) are considered to be very skillful in mimicry.

More drama with more serious content, emphasizing song and dance, replaced comedy and mimicry as time moved on into the Kamakura period. Actually, what happened was that the more serious Noh developed with music and dramatic dance, while comedy continued in the more discursive kyogen.

It was the famous father and son of Kan'ami and Zeami who really developed the Noh into an art form in the Muromachi period. From then on through the Edo period on up to the present, a Noh performance is always immediately followed by a kyogen performance. They are like fraternal twins. For even though they are very different, they have some essential similarities.

Noh has to be performed on a special stage with a roof. The main actor wears a *mask*: and all the performers wear ornate costumes. The mask is one device allowing for sudden transformation, and this kind of mask drama is found just about all over the world.

The players are the protagonist (shite almost wears the mask), the second, or supporting actor (waki does not wear a mask) and the musicians who play flute and drums (called

面，セリフが面白いばかりでなく，楽しい雰囲気に，私たちもつい引き込まれてしまいます。

　狂言は能と違って笑いを目的とする演劇ですから，現代の若者たちのフィーリングにも合うのでしょう。独立した演劇として高校などで演じられることもだんだん多くなってきたようです。

VOCABULARY　　*Sosho shite:* collectively called　　*Kokkei na:* humorous　　*Monomane:* mimicry　　*Buyogeki:* dance drama　　*Taiwageki:* discursive drama　　*Nohshozuku:* ornate costumes　　*Kamen:* mask　　*Suriashi:* sliding steps

hayashi). There is also a third actor, a companion or an assistant to the protagonist or the second actor (called the tsure).

There is no set in a Noh play. We are made to imagine a mountain or an earthquake from the chanting of the text (called utai), from the music, or from the movements of the actors.

This should be enough of an explanation for us now to go to a performance. You can hear the musicians. The shite enters in white tabi (socks with a separation between the big toe and the other toes) with sliding steps. This way of walking, sliding the feet along without lifting them off the ground is one of the most conspicuous features of a Noh performance. Do you think that way of walking is difficult? Well, if he is having difficulty, you would know it, because you can't see the actor's face behind his mask.

Now the Noh gives way to the kyogen performance, and suddenly the mood becomes relaxed, relieving the tensions of the Noh drama. On the stage the main actor is drunk and he's falling about. Not only the script is amusing as we are drawn into the atmosphere of fun.

Kyogen seems to be well-liked by today's young people because, in contrast to Noh, it aims to make the audience laugh. There has been an increase in independent performances of kyogen in high schools recently.

注

1. 観阿弥 (1333—1384)
   室町初期の能役者であり，謡曲の作者である。能楽観世流の始祖。
2. 世阿弥 (1363—1443)
   猿楽の伝統に幽玄を加えて，能楽を洗練するとともに，これに今日まで続いている芸術論の基礎を与えた。
3. 能面
   能では女性，老人，霊，超人間的な役にふんする時は必ず面をつける。
4. シテ方
   （主人公の役）　夢幻的，曲線的な演技。
5. ワキ方
   （主役の相手役）　現実的，直線的な演技。
6. 謡
   謡曲は「伊勢物語」「源氏物語」などの古典文学を主に，その他多くの伝承から取材して，「コトバ」と「フシ」で構成される。

3. 歌舞伎

日本の伝統芸術はいろいろありますが，その中でも歌舞伎は現在でも*大衆的な性格をもった演劇でしょう。人気のある*出し物の時には，歌舞伎座や国立劇場のよい席はいつでも売り切れてしまいます。

もしあなたが歌舞伎に興味をおもちなら，とにかく行ってみることです。観客はお弁当を食べながら*芝居の始まるのを待っていたりして，とても楽しそうな雰囲気です。

NOTES
1. *Kan'ami* (1333–1384) was a Noh actor in the early Muromachi period who wrote Noh plays. He was the founder of the Kanze school of Noh drama.
2. *Zeami* (1363–1443) added mystery to the sarugaku, refined the nohgaku and thereby developed the fundamental aesthetics of the Noh drama which persist today.
3. *Noh mask*: In the Noh, a mask must be worn for women, old people, spirits, or superhuman characters.
4. *Shite*: The protagonist, a dreamlike character, performed in an emotive and poetic fashion.
5. *Waki*: The subsidiary of the protagonist. His performance is realistic and rather dry.
6. *Utai*: The main Noh texts are classical literature like *the Tale of Ise* and *the Tale of Genji*, through there are many traditional stories too. The script is actually the words (kotoba) recited with in specific timings, called the fushi.

3. Kabuki

Japan has many traditional performing arts but amongst them it is Kabuki that maintains its character as the drama of the masses, even to the present day. Whenever a popular play is performed at the Kabuki-za or at the National Theatre, the best seats will always be sold out.

If you are interested in Kabuki, the best thing to do is to go and attend a performance; the spectators eating packed

中にはイヤホーンを耳に当てている人もいます。これは歌舞伎の解説を聞きながら芝居を見るもので、日本語のものと英語のものがあります。歌舞伎には決まりがたいへん多く、たとえば女形[1]の衣装一つを例にとっても、時代物の姫役は赤の大振りそで、山村漁村の村娘は緑地の衣装と解説がなければ分からないことも多いのです。

やがて幕が開きます。舞台の向かって左側に注目してください。ここは*下座といって歌舞伎の伴奏音楽を演奏しているところです。*長唄、三味線、*はやしと独得の節回しです。

さて舞台の上では役者たちによって芝居が進行していきますが、せりふの内容が理解できないからといって失望などしないでください。日本人にもなかなか聞き取りにくいのですから。

歌舞伎の舞台は、*回り舞台といって次の場面に素早く移り変われるように、舞台の床が丸く切り抜かれ、それが回るようになっていたり、*花道が観客席の中に設けられ役者の出入りが真近に見られるというふうにさまざまの工夫がこらされています。切符を買う時は花道に近い席を選ぶとよいですね。

隈取り[2]、*かつらなどもきっと皆さんの興味をひくでしょう。どんな化粧をしているかどんなかつらをつけているかで、大体その役柄が分かります。

歌舞伎は*様式美の世界です。感情が最高潮に達した時、役者が行動を停止し、まるで舞台が「絵」のような状態になります。これは「*見得」と言って、芝居によっていろいろな*名場面があります。

どうか歌舞伎を一度見てください。雰囲気を味わうことが、歌舞伎を理解する一番の近道ですから。

lunches, as they wait for the play to start, the atmosphere is one of people enjoying themselves.

Amongst the audience can be seen people with headphones. They are using the Earphone Guide Service which allows them to listen to a simultaneous commentary on the performance in either English or Japanese. Kabuki has many conventions. Taking the costume of the female impersonator as an example, a princess in a period or history play wears a scarlet kimono with long and elaborate sleeves. A girl from a mountain or fishing village, however, wears one of green. Without such simultaneous explanations, many spectators would be at a loss to understand.

When the curtain eventually opens, the first thing that is noticed is a room at the left-hand side of the stage. Called the geza, it is here that the musical accompaniment to a Kabuki play is performed. It has a distinctive style made up of nagauta singing to the accompaniment of the shamisen, drums and flute.

Meanwhile, on the main stage, the actors get on with the performance of the play. But do not despair if you cannot understand the content of the speeches because it is also difficult for the Japanese.

The Kabuki stage includes a number of elaborate devices. One is the revolving stage, a central, circular section, set in the main stage which, when rotated, allows for quick changes of scene. Another is the hanamichi ("flower path"), a narrow extension to the stage that runs through the audience

VOCABULARY *Taishuteki:* popular, appealing to the masses *Dashimono:* play *Shibai:* drama *Geza:* room at left of stage where accompanying music is performed *Nagauta:* a style of singing common in Kabuki *Hayashi:* ensemble of drums and flute *Mawari-butai:* revolving stage *Hanamichi:* " flower path " a narrow extension of the main stage to the back of the theatre *Katsura:* wig *Yoshikibi:* beauty of stylisation *Mie:* pose *Meibamen:* famous scene

注─────────────────────────────

1. 女形
   現代の歌舞伎はすべて男性で演じられる。女の役を演じる男性をいう。
2. 隈取り
   役者が表情を強く見せるため、顔に種々の色のしま模様を入れること。大体、赤系統の色は善人、青系統は悪人に使われる。

4. 着 物

外国人にとって日本の印象とはなんでしょう。富士山、桜に新幹線や*ハイテク産業、そして着物を着た日本女性ではないでし

to allow the actors' entrances and exits to be seen at close quarters. When buying tickets it is best to choose seats close to the hanamichi.

The kumadori makeup and wigs are other features that are bound to attract your attention. From the wig and makeup used it is possible to obtain a good idea of the type of role that is being performed.

Kabuki is a world of stylisation. When emotions are at their highest point, the actors pose standing perfectly still so that the stage becomes just like a picture. Such poses are called 'mie' and occur in a number of famous scenes.

Please try to see Kabuki at least once. The ability to appreciate its atmosphere is the best shortcut of all to understanding it.

NOTES
1. *Onnagata*: An actor who plays women's roles. Kabuki is performed exclusively by men.
2. *Kumadori*: In order to show the expression on his face more powerfully, the actor paints lines of various colours on his face. As a rule, red signifies good; blue, evil.

4. Kimono

The image that foreigners doubtless have of Japan is made up of Mt. Fuji, cherry blossoms, the Shinkansen Bullet Train,

ょうか。ところが実際に日本に来てみると，着物姿はほとんど見られず，皆が洋服を着ているのにがっかりしてしまう外国人も多いようです。

「美しい着物を着ないで，なぜ洋服を着るのですか。着物は日本の*民族衣装でしょう？」

これは外国人がかならず尋ねる質問です。

たしかに着物は見る人にとって美しいかもしれませんが，着る方にとっては大変なのです。まず人間の体は曲線的にできているのに着物は直線的で，特に幅の広い帯で体を*締めつけられると食事もできません。そで（たもと）は長く不自由で，床まであるすそは歩くのに不便です。「着物を着ると女らしくなる」と言われますが，それもそのはずで，着物を着るとゆっくりした動作しかできないのです。

なんだかこんなことばかり書いていると，着物を着たくないと思われるかもしれませんね。しかしそこが女心，たとえどんなに不自由でも，やはり美しいものは身につけたいのです。

お正月，成人式，結婚式，などの第一*礼装はやはり着物です。正装の時は絹の友禅染め[1]の着物が着られることが多く，その模様の美しさは一種の美術品とも言えます。

ふだん着に着物を着る人はだんだん少なくなっていますが，それでも年配の婦人がつむぎ[2]の着物で観劇に出掛けたりするのは，なにげないおしゃれでなかなかよいものです。

ゆかたは木綿でできた夏用の着物です。絹と違って洗濯も楽ですし，値段も手頃ですから，あなたもゆかたを着て盆踊りにでも出掛けてみませんか？ *素足に*げたをはくのも忘れずにね。

high technology and girls in kimono. But, to the regret of many of them if they eventually come to Japan, there are almost no kimono to be seen. Everybody wears western clothes.

"Why do Japanese women wear western clothes and not the beautiful kimono? Isn't it supposed to be the national dress of Japan?"

This is the kind of question that foreigners are likely to ask.

The kimono may be beautiful to look at but for the wearer it is hard work. The human body is curved but the kimono is straight. Also the wide obi sash is tightly tied which makes it difficult to eat. Movement is restricted because of the long sleeves and the long skirts which extend to the floor make it difficult to walk. It is often said that girls become more feminine in kimono but that is hardly surprising since they have no alternative but to walk slowly and elegantly.

Writing in this way may give the impression that Japanese women dislike wearing the kimono. On the contrary, it is a woman's nature to want to wear beautiful things however inconvenient they may be.

At the New Year, on Adults Day and at wedding ceremonies, the kimono is the formal garment of choice. On full dress occasions, it is usual to wear a kimono of printed (Yuzenzome) silk. The beauty of the pattern can make it into a work of art.

The number of people for whom the kimono is part of

VOCABULARY   *Haiteku sangyo:* high technology   *Minzoku isho:* national dress   *Shimetsukeru:* tie tightly   *Reiso:* formal wear   *Suashi:* barefoot   *Geta:* geta, wooden clogs

注
1. 友禅染め
   絹の布などに豊富な彩色で,人物,花鳥,草木,山水などの模様を染め出したもの。
2. つむぎ
   絹のつむぎ糸で織った絹織物。糸が太く,不ぞろいのため光沢はないが,控えめな美しさがある。一般にふだん着の着物に使われるが,製法の複雑なものは値段も高い。

5. 茶の湯

　茶の湯の*作法を茶道(さどう,ちゃどう)という。江戸時代中期以後に用いられるようになった言葉で,主として*抹茶の世界で用いられる。

　茶道を完成させたのは千利休(1522—1591)といわれている。戦国時代,豊臣秀吉[1]は堺の一町人であった利休に高禄を与えて*側近に仕えさせた。戦乱にあけくれた当時の人々の心を鎮めるためにも,茶道が*効果的だと考えたからだろう。それ以来,茶道は日本人の礼儀作法の一つとして受け継がれてきた。

their everyday wear is gradually decreasing. But an elderly married lady who goes to the Kabuki theatre in a kimono of plainly woven silk (Tsumugi) achieves a pleasing casual elegance.

The yukata is a kimono made of cotton. Unlike the silk kimono it is easy to wash and reasonable in price. It is often worn in summer at the O-Bon (All Souls) Festival together with geta clogs worn barefoot.

NOTES

1. *Yuzenzome*: Silk highly decorated in the Yuzen style with scenes flowers, birds, etc.
2. *Tsumugi*: A material made of thick threads of spun silk. Woven unevenly, it has no lustre but possesses a quality of restrained beauty. Kimono of tsumugi are worn for everyday use but, as the weaving is complicated, the cost is high.

5. Cha no Yu (The Tea Ceremony)

The art of the tea ceremony in Japan is called Sado or Chado (the way of tea). These are terms which came into use after the middle of the Edo Period and they refer mainly to the practice of preparing and drinking mattcha (powdered, whipped green tea).

The art of the tea ceremony is said to have been perfected by Sen Rikyu (1522–1591), a citizen of Sakai whom Toyotomi Hideyoshi made a personal attendant during the Sengoku

しかし最近は，日本間は洋間に，お茶はコーヒーにとってかわり，そして*嫁入り修業の一つに必ず加えられていた茶道も，ほんの一部の人たちのものになりつつある。あわただしい現代文明の中でこそ，私たちは静かなものを求める。茶道は日本的な特質をもつ芸術として，生き残るべきでしょう。

　茶室，茶道具，作法などは実際に体験してみるのが一番よい。百聞は一見にしかず。

VOCABULARY　　*Saho:* manners, etiquette　　*Mattcha:* cf. p. 15　*Sokkin:* personal attendant, close to　　*Kokateki:* effective　　*Yomeiri shugyo:* training for (a girl's) marriage

---

注

1. 豊臣秀吉 (1536—1598)
   戦国時代の武将，天下を統一した。

6. 生け花

　昔の生け花は「床の間」[1]という限られた場所に飾られるものだった。しかし現代ではホテルのロビー，駅や空港の待合室，デパートのショーウィンドーというようにいろいろな場所に飾られる

(Warring States) period, paying him a large remuneration. No doubt Hideyoshi was also of the opinion that the tea ceremony would be effective in calming the restless minds of the people. Since that time the tea ceremony has been handed down as one method of cultivating good manners and a sense of propriety in Japan.

Recently, however, the traditional Japanese room has been replaced by the western room and tea by coffee. The tea ceremony, which used to be a part of every girl's training for marriage, is now practised by only a few. But it is precisely because modern life is so hectic that people need peace and quiet. For its special Japanese qualities, the tea ceremony is an art that ought not to be allowed to die out.

Rather than simply read about it, the tea ceremony is better experienced for its etiquette and utensils and for the actual room in which it takes place.

NOTES

1. *Toyotomi Hideyoshi* (1536–1598): A general who unified the country during the Sengoku Period.

6. Ikebana (The Art of Flower Arrangement)

In former times examples of Ikebana were limited to decorating the toko-no-ma in people's houses. Nowadays, however, they can be seen on display everywhere including such places

ようになっている。

　*切り花の*消費量はアメリカが世界第一位，日本が第二位だが，日本の場合はそのほとんどが生け花に使われ，アメリカの量本位に花を飾ることとはかなり異なる。

　生け花とは，「花を通じて自己を表現する」と言われるように，外観の*装飾性よりも内容の精神性を大切にしている。それだからこそ「小原流」²「古流」³「草月流」⁴と考え方の違うさまざまな流派があり，*家元相互の競争心が生け花を現在のように発展させてきた。

　生け花界（華道界）は*門弟を底辺とし，家元を頂点としたピラミッド型の先生がその間にいるという組織で，外から見ると理解しにくい面もある。しかしどの流派にも共通することは「生きている草木を素材とする*瞬間芸術」であるということだ。つぼみは花に，そして花は 4～5 日もすれば枯れてしまう。

　この「芸術」がなぜこうも現代の日本人の心をひきつけるのだろうか。

VOCABULARY　　*Kiribana:* cut flowers　　*Shohiryo:* quantity, amount used, consumed　　*Soshokusei:* decorative qualities, decorativeness　　*Iemoto:* hereditary head or leader of a school of traditional Japanese art　　*Montei:* disciple, pupil, student　　*Shunkan geijutsu:* transitory, ephemeral art

as hotel lobbies, railway stations, airport lobbies and the windows of department stores.

America leads the world in the use of cut flowers with Japan second. But in Japan almost all cut flowers are used in Ikebana, an art very different from the floral decorations of America in which great emphasis is placed on the concept of quantity.

Ikebana is called "the expression of the self through flowers" which means that more importance is attached to the inner spiritual quality than to external, decorative effect. This explains why there are various schools of Ikebana such as the Ohara, the Ko and the Sogetsu. It is the spirit of mutual competition between the hereditary heads of these schools, over succeeding generations, that has made Ikebana what it is today.

The world of Ikebana or Kado (The way of flowers) is like a pyramid with the disciples or students at the base and the head of the school at the top. In between are the teachers or instructors. From the outside such organisations have features that are difficult to understand but what is common to all schools of Ikebana is "a transistory art that uses living flowers and plants". Buds blossom into flowers that themselves wither and die after four or five days.

What is it about this "transitory art" that continues, even today, to fascinate the hearts and minds of the Japanese?

注
1. 床の間
   日本座敷の床を一段と高くしたところ。壁に掛け物を掛け，床に花，置物などを飾る。
2. 小原流
   明治時代に創られた生け花の流派。現在の家元は三代目。その活動は国の内外に及んでいる。
3. 古流
   江戸時代中期に創られたもの。その自然さが一般に親しまれてきた。
4. 草月流
   昭和元年，勅使河原蒼風によって創られたもの。時代と共にかわる生け花を目指す。ガラス，軽金属などを使った「前衛生け花」は活動し続けている。

7. 盆　栽

　祖父の趣味は「盆栽」です。もう77歳で会社もとっくに定年退職しているので，1日の大部分の時間は盆栽の ために 使われます。

　庭の片隅に盆栽をのせた棚があります。その上にはたくさんの盆栽が*所狭しと並べられています。実際に数えたことはありませんが多分100以上あるでしょう。

　その中でも祖父のご*自慢のものは，樹齢500年もするエゾマツと，秋になるとたくさんの実をつける柿の木，そしてお正月にはいつも床の間に飾られる梅の木です。どれも高さ30cm くらいな

NOTES

1. *Toko-no-ma*: This refers to the alcove in a traditional Japanese room where the floor (toko) is raised slightly higher (compared to the rest of the room). The toko-no-ma is decorated with a hanging scroll on the wall or with some flowers or some artistic object on the floor.
2. *Ohara* School: Founded in the Meiji (1868–1911) period, the present head is the third to succeed to that position. The school is active both inside Japan and abroad.
3. *Ko* (Old) School: It was founded in the middle of the Edo Period (1603–1868). It is much favoured for its natural approach to the art of flower arrangement.
4. *Sogetsu* School: Created by Teshigawara Sofu, an "Imperial Messenger", it aims at a style of Ikebana that changes with the times. Using glass, metal and other materials, it continues as the "avant-garde" school of flower arrangement.

7. Bonsai (Miniature Trees)

My grandfather's hobby is bonsai, miniature trees. Now seventy-seven years old having retired long since, he spends most of his day working on his bonsai.

There are shelves all around his garden crowded with bonsai. I have never counted them, but I am sure there must be more than one hundred altogether.

His most prized bonsai are a silver fir, that is 500 years old, a persimmon tree that bears lots of fruit in the autumn, and a plum tree that always adorns the tokonoma at New Year.

のに、まるで大地に育ったように実に自然な姿をしています。

500歳のエゾマツは小さな鉢に植えられながら、まるで美しい日本庭園にあるようで、*荘厳な感じさえします。それに、こんな小さな鉢の中で、どうしてこんなにもたくさんの実が成り、花が咲くことができるのでしょう。不思議でなりません。

祖父に*秘けつを尋ねると、ニヤニヤしながら「愛情をこめて手入れしてやることだよ」と答えます。祖母は「盆栽におじいさんをとられましたよ」と言っていますが、盆栽に*焼きもちを焼いても仕方がありませんね。

きょうも祖父は熱心に鉢の植え替え[1]をしたり肥料[2]をやったり、小さな木の枝に針金を巻いて、整枝[3]したりしています。

「病気になった時には、盆栽の面倒を頼むよ」と祖父に言われていますが、とても自信がありません。

VOCABULARY　　*Tokoro semashi:* be crowded　　*Jiman no mono:* be prized　　*Sogon na:* solemnity　　*Hiketsu:* secret　　*Yakimochi o yaku:* be jealous

---

注
1. 植え替え
   新しい土に替え、活動力のない古い根を除いて新しい根を発生させる。常緑針葉樹類は5年に1回、花木、果樹類は毎年1回植え替える。
2. 肥料
   栄養を土に補給させるために、窒素、リン、骨粉などを与える。
3. 整枝

Though none of them is higher than thirty centimeters, their fruit look so much like the usual fruit, it is really quite amazing.

The five-hundred year old silver fir sits in its tiny pot. It has a solemnity that gives you the feeling of being in a beautiful Japanese garden. How on earth it bears so much fruit and so many flowers, I will never understand.

When I ask my grandfather for the secret to growing bonsai, he grins and says, "You just have to treat them with loving kindness." Grandmother says, "The bonsai have completely taken hold of me", but there is no point in being jealous of the bonsai, is there?

Today grandfather was working hard on transplanting bonsai, and fertilizing his trees, winding wire around their branches, and restoring them.

My grandfather says to me, "When I get sick, I want you to come and look after my bonsai," but I am not sure if I could do it properly.

NOTES
1. Transplanting: Removing old dead roots to allow new roots to grow and replanting the trees in new earth. Evergreen trees have to be transplanted once every five years, while flowering trees and fruit trees have to be transplanted once every year.
2. Fertilizing: Nitrogen, phosphorous, and bone meal are mixed into the earth to add nutrition for the little trees.
3. Restoration: Bonsai do not develop into beautiful trees if left

盆栽はそのままでは美しい姿となることはできない。幹や枝は針金を巻いて矯正し，必要のない枝はせん定する。

8. カタカナ・ひらがな

カタカナの「カタ」は*不完全という意味，平がなの「ひら」は「平易」（やさしい）という意味です。

カタカナは奈良時代末期から平安時代初期（8世紀～9世紀）日本で仏教が最も栄えた時代に，*僧りょが*仏典を研究する時，漢字の*略記号として使ったのがはじめと言われています。

ひらがなは万葉仮名¹を非常に*簡略化してできたものです。特に女性の間で発達したところから「女手」とも呼ばれ，平安時代の女性文学が発達する*きっかけになりました。

歌人として有名な紀貫之²は「古今和歌集³」に「*仮名序」を書き，和歌⁴が漢詩⁵と*対等の文学であることを*主張して，*後世に影響を与えました。

カタカナ，ひらがなが*現行のものに*統一されたのは，明治33年（1900年）のことです。

VOCABULARY　*Fukanzen:* incomplete, imperfect　*Soryo:* buddhist monk, bonze　*Butten:* buddhist writings, scriptures　*Ryakukigo:* abbreviated, simplified signs　*Kanryakuka:* abbreviation　*Kikkake:* opportunity, cause, start　*Kanajo:* preface written in kana　*Taito:* equal, equivalent to　*Shucho suru:* claim, assert　*Kosei:* posterity　*Genko:* present, existing　*Toitsu sareru:* to be united, unified

to themselves. The trunk and branches are wound with wire and the latter are set in the desired shapes, unnecessary branches are pruned.

8. Katakana and Hiragana

The "kata" of katakana means "incomplete" and the "hira" of hiragana comes from "heii" meaning simple.

Katakana is said to have begun in the late Nara and early Heian periods (8th to 9th centuries A.D.) as an abbreviated way of writing Chinese characters used by monks studying Buddhist scriptures when Buddhism was flourishing in Japan.

Hiragana evolved as an extremely simplified version of manyogana. Because it was in use largely amongst women, hiragana also became known as "women's hand" and provided the stimulus for the "women's literature" during the Heian Period.

The famous poet Ki no Tsurayuki wrote the preface to his *Kokin Waka Shu* in kana asserting that Waka (poems written in the native Japanese kana) were equal in literary value to Kanshi (poems in the Chinese style) and this has greatly influenced later generations.

The unification of katakana and hiragana in the present system of writing Japanese dates from 1900.

注──────────────────────────────
1. 万葉仮名
   日本語の音を表すのに，漢字を表音文字として表す他，訓も利用した表記法。
2. 紀貫之（?872-945）
   古今和歌集の中心的歌人，『土佐日記』の作者。
3. 古今和歌集
   20巻，1100余首，醍醐天皇（885-930）の勅命により作られた，はじめての勅撰和歌集。
4. 和歌
   31音（5・7・5・7・7）を定型とする短歌。
5. 漢詩
   中国の漢字で書かれた詩。

9. 百人一首

現代人である私たちに祖先が残してくれた*文学的遺産は多い。「百人一首」とは，百人の歌人の歌を*一首ずつ集めたもので，藤原定家[1]の撰と言われている。

これがかるた取り[2]という形をもったために，私たちの生活に深く入り込んだ。お正月の行事の一つとして，意味もわからないまま，百人一首を*暗唱した思い出をもつ日本人も多いと思う。

「百人一首」の歌の時代は古代から中世初期，つまり古代国家が*確立した天智天皇[3]の時代から皇室を中心とする貴族時代が終わる後鳥羽[4]，順徳天皇[5]の700年にわたっている。

恋の歌が43首と半分近くを占め，四季の歌が32首とそれに続いている。20世紀，欧米文化が私たちの生活を取り巻く中でも，百

108 V. 日本の文化

NOTES

1. *Manyogana*: A writing system in which Chinese characters were used phonetically to express both the "on" (Chinese) and "kun" (native Japanese) sounds of the Japanese language.
2. *Ki no Tsurayuki* (circa 872–945 A.D.): The principal poet in *the Kokin Waka Shu*. Author of *Tosa Nikki* (Tosa Diary).
3. *Kokin Waka Shu* (Collection of Poems Ancient and Modern): A collection of approximately 1100 poems in twenty volumes. It was compiled upon the order of the Emperor, Daigo (885–930). It was the first imperial poetry collection.
4. *Waka*: A short poem (tanka) of thirty-one syllables arranged in the order, 5, 7, 5, 7, 7.
5. *Kanshi*: Poems written in the Chinese style (i.e. solely with Chinese characters).

9. Hyakunin Isshu
(One Hundred Poems by One Hundred Poets)

The literary heritage left by our forebears to us who live in the present is very great. The Hyakunin Isshu is a collection of one poem each by a hundred famous poets and said to have been compiled by Fujiwara Teika.

These poems have an important place in the lives of the Japanese since they come in the form of a set of one hundred cards which are used in a game called karutatori. This is played in people's homes as an annual New Year' custom. As a result, there are doubtless many Japanese who can remember reciting the poems as they played although ignorant of their meaning.

V. Japanese Cultural Activities

人一首の心は生き続けている。

<u>久かたの</u> <u>光のどけき</u> <u>春の日に</u> (上の句)
　　5　　　　　7　　　　　5
　　<u>しづ心なく</u> <u>花の散るらん</u> (下の句)
　　　　7　　　　　　7

陽光がのどかな春の日なのに,桜の花は静かな心がなく,どうしてこのように散るのでしょうか,と作者,紀友則は惜しんでいる。

VOCABULARY　　*Bungakuteki isan:* literary heritage　　*Isshu:* one (Waka) poem　　*Ansho suru:* recite　　*Kakuritsu suru:* establish, found

---
注

1. 藤原定家（1162—1241）
2. かるた取り
   百人一首の場合,詠み手が「上の句」を詠み,「下の句」の書かれたカードが何枚とれるか競うもの。新年には「かるた会」がよく催される。
3. 天智天皇（626—671）

110　V. 日本の文化

The poems in the Hyakunin Isshu range from classical times to the early middle ages, i.e. the period of seven hundred years from the Emperor Tenchi, who created the Japanese nation, to the Emperors Gotoba and Juntoku with whose reigns came the end of the "aristocratic period" in Japanese history centered around the imperial family.

Forty-three of the poems in the Hyakunin Isshu are about love and thirty-two deal with the subject of the seasons of the year. Despite the overwhelming westernization of Japanese life in the twentieth century, the spirit of this ancient collection is still very much alive.

Hisakata no   Hikari nodokeki   Haru no hi ni (upper hemistich)
Shizu kokoro naku   Hana no chiru ran   (lower hemistich)

"While the sun's beams mellowly and peacefully flood this spring day, why are the restless cherry blossoms scattered so?"

Although it is a balmy spring day the poet, Kino Tomonori, regrets that the restless cherry blossoms scatter the way they do.

NOTES

1. *Fujiwara Teika* (1162–1241).
2. *Karutatori*: A game in which one person reads out the first half and the other players have to find the correct card with the second half written on it. Karuta-kai (Poem Card Tournaments) are often held at the New Year.
3. Emperor *Tenchi* (626–671).

4. 後鳥羽天皇 (1180—1239)
5. 順徳天皇 (1197—1242) 後鳥羽上皇の第3皇子。

10. 俳　句

　外国人に日本語を教えていると，文学好きの人は必ず「私も俳句を作ってみたいのですが，どんなことに注意すればいいのですか？」と聞きます。私はいつもこう言います。「俳句には2つの大切な約束があります。第1に1句の中に必ず季語が含まれていること，第2は使われる音数が17音で，しかも5音，7音，5音という3節から成り立っていることです。」

　こう説明すると，私たち日本人には予想もつかないような質問が出ます。「こがらしはなぜ冬なのですか？」たしかにタイやインドネシアのように一年中夏の国から来た学生にとっては，日本人の季節感，特に冬を表す季語は理解しにくいかもしれません。たった17音の短い詩でも，私たちはこがらしと聞いただけで，手足が凍るような寒さを連想します。耳元を吹き抜ける冷い風，凍りついた道，家で食べる暖いなべもの，今編みかけのマフラー，たった一つの言葉から連想は果てしなく広がっていくのです。文化的背景の違う学生にこれを理解してもらうには，「今年の冬が来たら，分かりますよ」と言うことにしています。

　もう一つの問題は音の数え方です。

　「先生，football は2音でいいですか？」

　「いいえ，フットボールは6音です」「え？」ただでさえ，促音や長音のように数えにくい音が多いのに，外来語を俳句に使う

4. Emperor *Gotoba* (1180–1239).
5. Emperor *Juntoku* (1197–1242): the third son of the Emperor Gotoba.

10. Haiku

As a teacher of Japanese, I am often asked by students interested in literature, "I want to try and write haiku myself, so what are the main things to keep in mind?" I usually tell them. "There are two important conventions in haiku. First, the poem must contain a seasonal reference and second, the number of syllables used must be exactly seventeen, the poem being composed of three lines of five, seven, and five syllables."

After this explanation, students often come up with questions which we Japanese would never imagine. For instance, "What does *kogarashi* (bitter cold wind) have to do with winter?" Certainly, it must be difficult for students from countries like Thailand and Indonesia, which enjoy summer weather almost all year round, to understand the Japanese perception of seasons, in particular words referring to winter. But even within the limitations of the seventeen syllables of haiku, when we hear only the word *kogarashi*, we immediately think of biting cold that gets to the hands and feet. Just this one word brings to mind cold winds that blow through our ears, frozen streets, homemade hot soups, and woolen scarves. I find that the only way to make foreign students

のはなおさら大変です。それでもその学生は，面白い俳句を作りました。

　フットボールや　けるあしもとに　桜ちる

　この句を見せてもらった時，彼の足元にひらひらと落ちたピンクの花びらと，それを見ている彼の情景を頭に描き感動してしまいました。彼が桜の花の季節を待っていたのを思い出しましたので。彼がここで，嬉しいとも言っていないのに，その情景から彼の気持ちが分かります。これが俳句の大切なところでしょう。
　俳句のよさはなんといっても，私たちが作者になれることです。これが小説などの他の文学と違うところですね。
（鑑賞）

菜の花や月は東に日は西に
　5　　7　　　5
　　　　蕪村（1716—1783）画家，俳人

　季語は菜の花，西の空に太陽が傾き，東の空には月が昇ってきています。黄色く一面に咲く菜の花畑，暖い春の夕方，本当に絵のような光景ですね。
　さあ，あなたも俳句を作ってみませんか。

with their different cultural backgrounds understand this is to say, "When winter comes this year, you'll learn."

A different problem is the method of counting the number of syllables.

"Is it all right to use football as two syllables?" I am asked.

I have to retort, "No it is not! In Japanese *futto-boru* has six syllables." The student is perplexed by this, and I have gone on to explain how to count double consonants and long vowels. This is just one of the various difficulties involved in using foreign loan words in haiku. Nevertheless, one student wrote a very interesting poem.

Futto-boru ya	(Kicking footballs,
keru ashimoto ni	cherry blossom leaves
sakura chiru	fall and stick to my shoes)

When he showed me this poem, I looked down at his shoes and saw the pink petals still there. The clarity of the impression of his sentiment imparted by this little poem was quite moving. I remembered that he had waited patiently for the cherry blossom season. The poem is no effusive expression of his joy or happiness, but there is plenty in it to let me appreciate his personal experience. This is also a very important part of a haiku.

Perhaps the finest thing about haiku is that it is relatively easy to write. This is its distinguishing feature with novels

11. 書　道

　白い紙に*墨で黒々と書く「書道」という芸術は，忙しい時にも気持ちを落ち着かせてくれる。

　書道用具には，*筆，*すずり，墨，紙，手本，下敷，*文鎮，水差しなどがある。

　書道は中国から伝わった「*経(きょう)」を写すこと[1]から始まった。そして平安時代に仮名が発明された結果，中国とは趣の違う仮名書道が発達した。長い歴史の中で，名筆[2]と呼ばれてきた古典の書が，今も私たちの目を楽しませてくれる。現在「書道」は国語教育の中に取り入れられ，日本人ならだれでも，筆を持って白い紙に向かい*緊張した経験をもつことだろう。

and other literary forms.

> Na no hana ya Mustard flowers
> tsuki wa higashi ni the moon is in the east
> hi wa nishi ni the sun in the west
>> Buson (1716–1783), painter and poet.

Na no hana is the seasonal reference, the sun has moved over to the western sky, and the moon is rising in the east. The simple poem immediately conjures in minds images of wide fields of blooming mustard flowers, a warm spring evening. The imagery of this poem is close to painting, don't you think?

Now, wouldn't you like to try writing a haiku?

11. Shodo (Calligraphy)

Shodo is the art of writing Chinese characters in black, chinese ink. Its practice helps to calm one at busy times.

The equipment necessary for Shodo includes brush, ink stone, ink stick, paper, copy book, felt underlay (on which to rest the paper), paper weight and water container.

Shodo started with the copying of Buddhist sutras brought to Japan from China. Then in the Heian Period, as a result of the invention of kana, there developed kana shodo, a style different in appearance to that of China. Even after many centuries, the ancient calligraphy of the so-called Meihitsu is

よい字を書くにはよいお手本をたくさん見ること、そしてたくさん練習することだそうである。最近*展覧会などで見る作品の中には、絵のようで、日本人にも読めない「書」がある。伝統を重んじてきた書道も「個性を尊重する」時代に入ったといえるのかもしれない。

VOCABULARY　*Sumi*: Chinese (Indian) ink　　*Fude*: brush　*Suzuri*: ink stone　*Bunchin*: paperweight　*Kyo*: sutra　*Kincho*: strain, stress　*Tenrankai*: exhibition

注
1. 経を写すこと（写経）
　日本では7世紀の終わりごろ仏教が国家的に取り上げられたことから、テキストとして必要な経典制作のため、写経が盛んに行われた。また経典（法華経）には写経することにより功徳があると書かれている。
2. 名筆
　三筆（平安時代）嵯峨天皇、空海、橘逸勢
　三蹟（平安時代）小野道風、藤原佐理、藤原行成

12. やきもの

　デパートなどで催される「やきもの展」などに出掛けたことがありますか？　日本各地で発達したやきものの種類の多さ、その

a delight to behold. Nowadays, Shodo has been adopted into the educational system so that any Japanese, no matter who, will have experienced the tension of facing a blank piece of paper, brush in hand.

To write Chinese characters well, it is necessary to study many copy books and to practise hard. Recently there have been many examples of calligraphy shown in exhibitions that are so pictorial in execution that even Japanese people are unable to read them. Perhaps it can be said that even Shodo, despite the great tradition behind it, has entered the age of individuality.

NOTES

1. Copying Buddhist Sutras: At the end of the seventh century, A.D. Buddhism was adopted by the state. Copying sutras became widespread as a means of producing the necessary sacred texts. Copying Buddhist scriptures like the Lotus Sutra was also thought to be means of acquiring merit.
2. *Meihitsu* (Famous Calligraphers): *Sanpitsu* (The three famous calligraphers of the Heian Period, 9th Century): the Emperor Saga, Kukai and Tachibana no Hayanari. *Sanseki* (The three great calligraphers of the Heian Period, 10th Century): Ono no Michikaze, Fujiwara Sukemasa and Fujiwara Yukinari.

12. Pottery and Ceramics

Have you ever visited a pottery exhibition held in a department store or similar place? In Japan, the many types of

*微妙な色の違いに驚かされます。

陶器¹は鎌倉時代に中国から技術が伝わったものです。茶の湯の発達とともに各地に*かまが作られ、日本独得の素朴なやきものが生まれ育ちました。土の種類、火の温度、*うわぐすりの使い方などによって、荻焼き、薩摩焼き、織部焼き、志野焼き、信楽焼き、益子焼きなどと個性的なやきものができます。これらは和風の食器にもよく使われます。特に名工の手になる手作りの食器などは、どこからか人の暖かさが伝わってくるような気がします。

磁器²は17世紀の初め、朝鮮の職人によって有田で作られ始めます。その後美しい色のついた絵がつけられ、オランダとの貿易を通じてヨーロッパにも輸出されます。江戸時代後半から日常の茶わんや皿がこの方法によってたくさん作られるようになりました。現在の日本人の家庭でも大半は磁器（有田焼き、清水焼き、瀬戸焼き）が使われています。

日本の陶磁器工業はその大部分が輸出に頼っています。輸出先はアメリカが主で、洋食器、おもちゃなどです。

日本の陶磁器の輸出額	1984……239,684（単位百万円）
	1985……222,591
	1986……172,311

（内訳）　（1986年12月）

飲食器	71,481	置物，装飾品	26,507
タイル	18,503	電磁器	23,741
その他			

　　　　　　　　　　　　　　　　　　（注）　日本陶業連盟調べ

VOCABULARY　　*Bimyo:* subtle　　*Kama:* kiln, vessel
Uwagusuri: glaze

ceramic ware, all with subtle differences in their colouring, are truly remarkable.

The technique of making glazed pottery was brought to Japan from China during the Kamakura Period. With the development of the tea ceremony, kiln and vessels for containing hot water were produced all over the country and, in the process, Japanese-style ceramics came into existence with its characteristic simplicity of form. According to the clay used, the temperature of firing and method of glazing, such distinctive types were created as Hagi, Satsuma, Oribe, Shino, Shigaraki and Mashiko ware. Many examples come in the form of Japanese traditional-style kitchen ware. When the work of craftsmen, this kind of hand made pottery conveys, somehow, a sense of human warmth and care.

Chinaware began to be made in Arita by Korean craftsmen. Subsequently, through trade with Holland, Japanese pottery decorated with beautiful pictorical scenes was also exported to Europe. In the latter half of the Edo Period, china was widely used for tea bowls and dishes. At present, half the ceramic ware used in people's houses is china (porcelain), Arita, Kiyomizu and Seto ware, etc.

The Japanese ceramics industry is largely dependant on export. Most of these exports are destined for the United States in the form of kitchen ware and toys.

注

1. 陶器
   厚手にできていて、透光性はない。
2. 磁器
   薄手の食器に適する。透光性があり、上絵(うわえ)によって多くの色を出すことができる。

NOTES

1. *Toki*: Pottery is thick and not translucent.
2. *Jiki*: China and porcelain, being thin and translucent, are highly suitable for external decoration.

Ⅵ. スポーツ（相撲, 柔道, 野球）

1. 相 撲

　東京の両国に新国技館がある。1985年に建てられたもので相撲の*殿堂とでもいったらよいだろうか。一年に6回ある本場所のうち3場所, つまり, 初場所（1月）, 夏場所（5月）, 秋場所（9月）はここで, また春場所（3月）は大阪, 名古屋場所（7月）は名古屋, 九州場所（11月）は福岡で行われる。

　もし興味をおもちなら, ぜひ相撲を見に行かれるとよい。人気のある日本の*国技だけによい席はすぐに売り切れてしまう。「百聞は一見にしかず」のことばどおり, どんなに後ろの席でもテレビで見るよりはずっと楽しめるだろう。

　競技の場になる土俵[1]に, 力士が登場した。普通の日本人よりずっと大きい。力士になるためには義務教育を終えた者で, 身長173cm, 体重75kg 以上なければいけないそうだ。もちろん体格がよいだけでは力士になれない。つらい練習を重ねて, やっと土俵に上がることができるのだ。力士はいつもまげ[2]を結っている。そして土俵にあがる時には, 腰のまわりに色あざやかなまわしを締める。レスリングやボクシングのように*体重制限というものがないから, やせた力士と山のように大きな力士が対戦することもある。力士は一場所, 15日間を毎日違う相手と*対戦し, でき

VI. Sports (sumo, judo, baseball)

1. Sumo

The New National Sports arena is in Ryogoku in Tokyo. Construction was completed in 1985, and this arena is the shrine of Japanese sumo wrestling. Three of the six tournaments held each year take place there. They are the first tournament, in January, the summer tournament, in May, and the autumn tournament, in September. The others are the Spring tournament in March, held in Osaka, the Nagoya tournament, in July, and the Kyushu tournament in November, in Fukuoka.

It is a fascinating experience to go to visit one of the tournaments of this very popular Japanese national sport. The good seats sell out soon, but as the saying goes, "one look is worth a thousand words," and no matter how far back your seats may be, it is much more fun to see it live than on television.

The wrestlers fight in the ring, on a mound built of clay. The wrestlers are much bigger than the average Japanese. They must have finished their compulsory education over 173 centimeters in height, and more than 75 kilogrammes in weight to

るだけたくさんの*白星をあげるように努力するのだ。

　勝負に入るまでには，昔から伝えられた慣習[3]どおりしこを踏み，清めのための塩をつかんで土俵上に振りまく。幕内力士[4]の立ち合いの制限時間は4分に決められている。

　力士が立ち上がる。立ち上がった以上は，力士の足裏以外の体のどの部分でも，土に触れれば負けである。勝敗は技[5]によって*行司(ぎょうじ)が決める。あっという間に勝敗が決定することもあれば，2人の実力が*互角で，2分間も勝負のつかないこともある。

　*審判は，ほとんどが軍配を手にした土俵上の行司によってされるが，土俵下にも5人の審判委員がいる。行司の審判に*不服がある時は5人の審判委員で話し合い，*ビデオ判定されることもあり，時には勝負のやり直しになることもある。

　地方に住んでいて，なかなか本場所を見に行けない人のために地方巡業が行われる。そこに行くのも無理な人はテレビで観戦するとよい。

　このごろでは，外国人にも*熱狂的なファンがいる。ここ当分，相撲の人気は衰えることがないだろう。

VOCABULARY　*Dendo:* shrine　*Kokugi:* national sports　*Taiju seigen:* weight classes　*Taisen suru:* fight　*Shiroboshi:* victories　*Gokaku:* evenly matched　*Shinpan:* judges　*Gyoji:* referee　*Fufuku ga aru:* unclear　*Bideo hantei:* video playbacks　*Nekkyo teki na:* enthusiastic

qualify as sumo wrestlers. Of course, it is not enough just to have a good physique. They have to undergo long, exacting training before they get to climb into the ring. They have to wear their hair in the characteristic topknot at all times, not just during the tournaments. When they climb into the ring they wear the colorful loincloth and belt wound around the waist. There are no weight classes as in wrestling and boxing, so slimmer wrestlers have to fight against the big heavy ones. Each wrestler fights a different opponent each day of the fifteen day tournament with the goal being to achieve the most overall victories.

According to an ancient custom, each wrestler takes a fistfull of salt and throws it in the air toward the center of the ring to consecrate as they stamp on it. The build up to the fight lasts a maximum of four minutes for the Makuuchi wrestlers.

The wrestlers lurch towards each other as they rise to the fight. If any part of the body of a wrestler other than the soles of his feet touches the ground, then he loses. Victory is awarded by the referee by announcing the technique that secured it. Sometimes fights last only a few seconds, but some fights last as long as two minutes if the wrestlers are evenly matched.

The fight is regulated by the referee in the ring, almost always with his flat fan in his hand, but there is also a committee of five judges sitting at ringside. The committee inter-

注

1. 土俵
   直径 455cm の円形の平面で，円の外は 545cm の正方形で囲まれ，高さ 34cm～60cm の固めた粘土でできている。表面には砂をまく。
2. まげ
   江戸時代，力士は武士と同じようなまげを結ったが，今でもその伝統が受け継がれている。
3. 昔から伝えられた慣習
   日本の相撲は古事記や日本書紀に出てくる神話時代から始まる。その後，奈良時代は朝廷行事として定着し，鎌倉時代には武士に奨励され，江戸時代には職業力士まで登場している。
4. 幕内力士
   力士は上位から，横綱，大関，関脇，小結，前頭までを幕内という。
5. 技
   技は48手（技法）ある。

venes if the decision is unclear, and they sometimes use video playbacks to determine the victor. They may order a rematch in some cases.

Provincial tours are also held to give those fans who cannot get to the big tournaments a chance to see the wrestlers in action, but many people watch the fights live on television.

There are often many enthusiastic foreign fans at the tournaments. Sumo will probably remain popular for a long time to come.

NOTES

1. The ring: The ring is 455 centimeters in diameter set on a 545 centimeter square mound, which is 34 to 60 centimeters high, built of hardened clay. The surface of the ring is covered with sand.
2. The topknot: In the Edo period the wrestlers were required to dress their hair in the same kind of topknot as the samurais, and this tradition is continued today.
3. Sumo is mentioned in the ancient Japanese books, the *Kojiki* and the *Nihon Shoki*, beginning in prehistoric times. It was firmly established as a court ceremony in the Nara period, and was supported by the samurai in the Kamakura period. Professional wrestler appeared in the Edo period.
4. *Makuuchi wrestlers*: This is the top division of sumo wrestlers. From the highest rank, the wrestlers are classified into grand champions (yokozuna), champions (ozeki), junior champions (sekiwake), the fourth rank called komusubi, and the fifth and largest rank, maegashira.
5. Techniques: There are forty-eight different techniques.

2. 柔 道

　柔道は現在世界のすみずみまで*普及し，国家，人種を問わず，多くの人々に愛されている。国際柔道連盟への加盟が100か国を超えた。なぜこれほど柔道は世界の人たちに愛されているのだろうか。

　柔道の特長は「柔(じゅう)よく剛を制す」ということばに表れている。これは弱い者でも強い者に勝つことがあるという意味で，相手の力を上手に利用すれば，強い相手でも倒すことができるのだ。

　これまでオリンピックで日本以外でも韓国や西ドイツ，ロシア，フランスの選手たちが金メダルを手にしている。このことは実力面でも柔道がすでに日本の柔道から，世界の柔道になったことを示している。

　現在世界の柔道人口は600万人といわれるが，そのうち100万人は外国人である。夕方，講道館(こうどうかん)を訪れると，多くの日本人に*混って外国人たちが技[1]を磨いている。柔道をよく知らない人でも，帯の色[2]で実力の見当がつく。

VOCABULARY　　*Fukyu suru:* spread, extend (intr.)　　*Majiru:* be mixed, mingled with

2. Judo

At the present time, Judo has spread to the four corners of the globe and is enjoyed by multitudes of people irrespective of country and race. The number of countries affiliated with the International Judo Federation exceeds one hundred. Why is it that Judo has attracted so much interest throughout the world?

Judo's main feature lies in the principle, "The flexible controls the hard" (Ju yoku Go o seisu) which means that the weak can defeat the strong. In Judo, therefore, it is possible for the weaker opponent to win if he can use the other's strength skilfully to his own advantage.

In the Olympic Games, competitors from various countries, other than Japan (S. Korea, W. Germany, Russia and France) have won gold medals in Judo. This demonstrates that, even from the point of view of ability, Japanese judo has now become world Judo.

The number of people currently practising Judo throughout the world is said to be 6,000,000 of which 1,000,000 are non-Japanese. A visit to the Kodokan International Judo Center will reveal large numbers of foreign students mingling with the Japanese and polishing their technique. Even those unfamiliar with Judo can judge a person's ability by the colour of the belt he or she wears.

注
1. 技
   代表的な技だけでも80種類くらい。
2. 帯の色
   白帯　初心者　　茶帯　1，2，3級　　黒帯　初段〜5段
   紅白帯　6〜8段　　赤帯　9〜10段。

3. 野　球

　日本人がこよなく愛するスポーツは野球である。

　8月に海外に出た人は日本の新聞をとても読みたがる。それは甲子園球場で行われている高校野球[1]の結果が気になるからだ。家庭では昼間からテレビの前に*釘づけになり，*地元の高校を*応援する。

　野球をする少年たちにとって，甲子園で戦うことは大きな夢なのだ。そして甲子園のスターたちは大学野球あるいはプロ野球にスカウトされる者もいれば，ただの野球愛好者になる者もいる。

　日本のプロ野球は12球団で，セリーグ[2]とパリーグ[3]に分かれる。それぞれがペナントを競って130試合を戦う。*開幕のときはどのチームも同じスタートラインだ。目的は一つ，リーグで*優勝すること。しかし優勝できるのは1チームだけ。そして勝ったチームが日本シリーズで戦う。この時は日本中が野球狂になったかと思うほどで，優勝したチームのオーナーがデパートの場合は，大バーゲンセールが展開される。

　この人気の*秘密は何なのだろうか。野球はビジネスであり，競技であり，見せるスポーツである。そこには集団の中での協

NOTES

1. Techniques: Standard techniques alone come to about eighty.
2. Belt Colours in Judo: White belt—beginners, Brown belt—3-1 Kyu, Black belt—1-5 Dan, Red and white belt—6-8 Dan, Red belt—9-10 Dan.

3. Baseball

The sport the Japanese love above all others is baseball.

In August, people who have gone abroad become very impatient to read Japanese newspapers. The reason is that they are anxious to know the results of the high school baseball championship held at Koshien stadium. As for people in their homes, they remain riveted to their television sets from midday onwards, cheering on their local teams.

For young baseball players, to compete at Koshien is their greatest dream. Some Koshien stars even go on to become university or professional players; others to be or just ordinary baseball fans.

Japanese professional baseball consists of twelve teams divided into the "Se" (Central) League and "Pa" (Pacific) League. They compete for a pennant in one hundred and thirty matches. When the curtain goes up on the season, every team is on the same starting line. Their aim is the same. To be the league winner. But only one team can win. Then the

力, 勤勉, 年功序列, *メンツなどを重視する日本人社会の特徴がすべて入っている。しかしプラス・アルファーが何であるのか私には分からない。

VOCABULARY *Kugizuke:* nailed, riveted *Jimoto:* local, home *Oen:* cheer, support, root for *Kaimaku:* opening of the curtain, start *Yusho:* victory *Himitsu:* secret *Mentsu:* face

注
1. 高校野球
   夏の全国高等学校野球選手権大会。
2. セントラルリーグ
   1950年創立, 加盟チーム, 読売ジャイアンツ, 阪神タイガース, 中日ドラゴンズ, 横浜大洋ホエールズ, 広島東洋カープ, ヤクルトスワローズの6球団。
3. パシフィックリーグ
   1950年創立, 阪急ブレーブス, 近鉄バッファローズ, 日本ハムファイターズ, 南海ホークス, 西武ライオンズ, ロッテオリオンズの6球団。

winning teams of each league compete in the Japan Series. At this time the whole of Japan seems to be baseball mad and if the owner of the eventual winning team is a department store, grand bargain sales are immediately held.

What is the secret of this popularity? Baseball is a business, a contest and a spectator sport. Group cooperation, application, seniority rule, "face", every important feature of Japanese society is contained in it. But what there is beyond that I do not know.

NOTES

1. High School Baseball: The summer National Inter-High School Baseball Tournament.
2. The Central League: Established in 1950, it is made up of six teams: The Yomiuri Giants, The Hanshin Tigers, the Chunichi Dragons, The Yokohama Taiyo Whales, The Hiroshima Toyo Carp and The Yakult Swallows.
3. The Pacific League: Established in 1950, it comprises The Hankyu Braves, The Kintetsu Buffaloes, The Nihon Ham Fighters, The Nankai Hawks, The Seibu Lions and the Lotte Orions.

Ⅶ. 日本歴史の旅

　皆さん，こんにちは。今日は皆さんをタイムカプセルに乗せて，「日本歴史の旅」にご案内したいと思います。これは時間と空間を乗りこえて，過去の世界に皆さんをお連れするものです。カプセルの中は安全ですし，過去の世界の人たちに私たちの姿は見えませんから，どうぞご安心ください。では出発します。シートベルトをお締めください。

1.　原始社会

①　石器時代
　今から13万年前から1万年前までの約12万年も続いた長い時代です。みんなの*暮らしぶりを窓からよく見てください。狩猟をしたり，食べものを探して暮らしています。動物を捕まえたり，海や川では魚や貝をとっていますね。集団生活はあまり見られません。人々が一か所に固まると，まわりに食べるものがなくなってしまうので，家族単位で暮らしています。階級もなければ，もちろん富の力を基礎とする権力もない，これが原始社会の特徴です。

VOCABULARY　　*Kurashiburi:* life styles

VII. Journey through Japanese History

Hello everyone. We're about to begin a journey through Japan's past. Enclosed in the Time Traveller, you'll be safe, and the people of the past won't be able to see us or the ship, so relax as you take in the sights and sounds. It's time to take off. Fasten your seat belts everybody!

1. Primitive Society

(1) Stone Age

Japan's Stone Age began 130,000 years ago. It was a very long period, lasting 120,000 years. Take a good look at the life styles of the Stone Age people from your window. They lived by hunting and gathering food. You can see them hunting animals and catching fish in the rivers and along the coast, where they are also collecting shellfish. You'll notice that there are no settlements of people living together in groups. If they did that, the food around them would soon be used up, so they live separately in family units. There are no social classes, and of course, no power built on wealth. This is a characteristic feature of primitive society.

② 縄文土器時代

　紀元前8000年から紀元前300年。人々は土器に縄の模様を付け始めます。この長い年代に様式はだんだん複雑なものに変化しています。

2. 古代社会初期 (弥生文化の誕生)

　紀元前300年に始まり約600年続きます。弥生文化は縄文とはまったく違った文化をもち，弥生式土器は高温で焼かれた薄手なものです。ここは日本の南の島，今の北九州です。人々は稲の*栽培を始めています。日本人の祖先が10万年もの長い間，石器文化の中で*足踏みをしていた時，大陸ではもう金属文化の時代で強力な国家を作っています。大陸の影響を受けて，この地で初めて金属器が使われ始め，*水田耕作も始まるのです。

　弥生文化は今までの日本社会の構造を*一変させました。

　窓から見てください。人々は水田耕作のために共同労働するようになり，どうやら階級関係まで生まれているようですね。住む家まで違っています。高床の住宅は支配階級，竪穴は一般民衆のものです。

　日本の中にこうした集団が100以上もあります。その中でも邪馬台国の女王「卑彌呼」¹の力は強いようです。たくさんの人々が従っていますね。彼女の*呪術の能力がそのまま政治的な*統制力になっているのでしょう。

(2) Jomon Period

From 8,000 B.C. to 300 B.C. The people have begun to produce stoneware pottery decorated with straw-rope patterns. This is a more complex culture and you can see the many changes over this long period.

2. Beginning of Ancient Society (Birth of Yayoi Culture)

In the third century B.C., Yayoi society continues for about 600 years. Yayoi culture is quite different from that of the Jomon Period. Yayoi style pottery is baked at high temperatures and is thin. We are now in northern Kyushu, Japan's southern island. Look, the people have begun to cultivate rice. While the ancestors of the Japanese marked time during the hundred thousand years of Stone Age culture, over on the continent a powerful state had grown up based on a culture of iron and other metals. That's where the metal utensils these people are using first came from, and with them the idea of irrigation for those paddy fields.

Yayoi culture effects enormous changes in the life of the people of Japan.

You can see from your window that rice cultivation requires that the people work together in the paddy fields, and as you can also see, class divisions are developing. The floors in the houses of the rulers are raised above ground, while the general

VOCABULARY *Saibai:* cultivation *Ashibumi o suru:* mark time *Suiden Kosaku:* irrigation of paddy fields *Ippensaseru:* make enormous changes *Jujutsu:* magic *Toseiryoku:* force of political control

注─────────────────────────────
1. 卑彌呼
「魏志倭人伝」(3世紀ごろの日本に関する中国の文献に,邪馬台国の女王卑彌呼が「鬼道につかえてよく衆を惑わし」とある。)

3. 律令社会

3世紀末から4世紀はじめ,大和政権が成立します。舞台は北九州から,本州の大和(今の奈良県)に移ります。

7世紀のはじめ,国政を担当しているのはあの有名な聖徳太子(574~622)です。ここで少し彼の仕事ぶりをみてみましょう。

仏教は日本に伝わってから,まだ数十年たったばかり,でも太子が仏教を重んじたので,あちこちに仏像が造られ寺院が建てられています。

冠位12階の制定により,身分は今までのように家柄で決めるのではなく,個人の功績によって決まります。そのほかにも17条の憲法を定めたり,隋(中国,581~618)と国交を開始したり,すばらしい仕事をしています。タイムカプセルをもうちょっと進め

population lives in dugouts in the ground.

There are more than one hundred of these communities throughout Japan at this time. Among them, Queen Himiko of Yamatai seems to be very powerful, with many subjects under her. Her secrets of divination and magic are a powerful force of political control.

NOTES
1. Himiko: The *Gishi Wajin Den*, a Chinese account of Japan in the third century A.D., states that Queen Himiko of Yamatai ruled the people by magic.

3. Society Based on Law

We have moved from northern Kyushu to Yamato, now Nara prefecture on the main island of Honshu, where political unity is established in Japan around the end of the third century A.D.

At the beginning of the seventh century, part of the country is being run by the famous Shotoku Taishi (574–622). Let's take a look at the work of this remarkable man.

Only a few decades have elapsed since Buddhism entered Japan. But Taishi has great respect for the new religion, and under his influence images of Buddha are produced and temples built in many places.

てみましょう。

　7世紀の中ごろになると,中国の*律令機構が日本にも*根をおろします。律令とは簡単に言うと,人民を中央政府が統一的に支配するものです。

　窓から働く人々の姿を見てみましょう。人々は政府から一定の田が与えられましたが,生活は決して楽ではないようですね。重い税金と労働のために, 人々はまるで*奴隷のようです。この律令社会は平安時代の初期,つまり9世紀ぐらいまで続きますが,*荘園の発達でこの制度は少しずつ崩れてきます。だれだって奴隷のように働かされるのはいやですから, 貴族や寺社の*私有地である荘園に逃げ込む人が多かったのです。たくさんの貴族の中でも藤原氏の力は特にすごいですね。

　しばらくは,藤原氏*独裁の貴族政治の時代です。

　あそこに見えるのは,平安京と呼ばれる都(現在の京都)です。*区画がきちんとし,整然とした街なみをごらんください。*朝廷の家を中心に*貴族たちの家が並んでいますね。

VOCABULARY　　*Ritsuryo kiko:* legal system　　*Ne o orosu:* put down roots　　*Dorei:* slaves　　*Shoen:* manor　　*Shiyuchi:* private ownership　　*Dokusai:* despotism　　*Kukaku:* sections　　*Chotei:* court　　*Kizoku:* aristocrats

He introduces a system of twelve court ranks, determined not by family or ancestors, but by the talents and skills of the individual. Here is his constitution of seventeen articles. He also opens direct communications with the Sui dynasty in China (581–618). These are just some of the achievements he is famous for. Let's take the Time Traveller on forward a bit.

As we reach the middle of the seventh century, we can see that the ideas underlying the legal system of China have established roots in Japan. A unified system of law maintained by the authority of the central government is still relatively recent here in Japan.

Let's have a look from our windows at how the ordinary people work at this time. They are given a fixed area of rice fields to work by the government, but this does not mean that they have it easy. Why, they are more like slaves, the way they have to work to meet the heavy tax and labor requirements. This society continues up to the beginning of the Heian period, that is to the beginning of the ninth century. It is slowly undermined by the development of the manors. Nobody wants to work like a slave, so it is not surprising that we can see many people fleeing to the manors owned by nobles, temples and shrines. The most powerful of the nobles are the Fujiwara family.

For a while there is a period of aristocratic government, which is called the Fujiwara despotism.

4. 貴族社会

平安京とその中に住む貴族たちの生活をのぞいてみましょう。平安京という都の中で，実際の政治から遠のき，趣味の世界の中で*優雅に生きています。地方の農村ではあいかわらず人々の貧しい暮らしがありますね。でも貴族たちは荘園の管理さえも地方官に任せて，都から出ようとはしません。まるで鎖国のような生活です。

貴族文化は支配階級の物質的に恵まれた条件の中から生まれたものです。この時代は日本文化が花開いた時で，源氏物語のような物語文学，和歌，そして数々の日記などが書かれました。また貴族の家の障子やびょうぶには大和絵（日本画）が描かれ，それらは今でも博物館に保存されています。この貴族文化は11世紀ごろになると，都を離れて地方にも*浸透していきます。日本文化が高度に*成熟していく様子がよくわかりますね。

VOCABULARY　　*Yuga:* elegance　　*Shoji:* window covers
Byobu: screens　　*Shinto suru:* spread　　*Seijuku:* maturity

Here is the capital of the new society, called Heiankyo (now Kyoto), with its clearly defined districts and orderly street layout. The mansions of the nobles are over there around the imperial palace at the center of the city.

4. Aristocratic Society

Now we are in a good position to have a look at the aristocratic way of life in the ancient capital. The aristocrats live a life of elegance and refinement far removed from the cares of the world and real politics. Their estates in the country are managed for them by others, because they can't tear themselves away from the pleasures of life in the capital. They live in their own exclusive little world, quite literally a closed society.

Aristocratic culture was born within the climate of material prosperity of the ruling classes. This is the golden age of Japanese culture when tales (such as the Tale of Genji), poems (like the collections of waka poetry), and diaries are written. Some of the pictures of ancient Japanese life you can see down there on the shoji window covers and screens are still preserved in our museums today. As we move on to the eleventh century, this aristocratic culture has spread to the rural areas beyond the capital. It's a treat to see the exceptional heights, the maturity of Japanese culture.

5. 封建社会の成立

　私たちのタイムカプセルは貴族社会から武士の社会へと動いていきます。

　平安時代の中ごろ以後になると，農業生産力の上昇に裏付けられた有力者が成長し，武士が育っていきます。自分たちの土地を守り，勢力を強めるために武士たちは弓矢や刀で武装し，馬に乗って戦っています。強い主従関係で結ばれた武士たちは小さなまとまりから，しだいに大きな武士団になっていきます。

　11世紀の後半です。東北地方では次々に大きな戦いが起こっていますね。その中で武士を率いて戦いを鎮めているのが源氏です。同じ武士でありながら平氏は，それまで貴族たちによって占められていた高い地位を京都で得るようになります。

　1185年，有名な「壇ノ浦の源平合戦」です。このカプセルの中から戦いの様子を眺めてみましょう。おびただしい船の数です。数えられませんね。実際には海上で戦う武士たち，平氏500，源氏840の船です。ついに平氏は源氏に滅ぼされます。

　1192年，ここはもう一つの都，鎌倉です。平氏を滅ぼしたあと，源頼朝は鎌倉に*幕府を開きます。江戸時代まで約700年間続く*武家政治の初まりです。頼朝は家来の武士たちを*統率するための政治の仕組みを作り出しました。しかしいぜんとして京都の朝廷は強い力を持ち続けています。

　カプセルはしばらく戦いの中を進みます。天皇に味方する武士たちによって鎌倉幕府は倒されます。そのあとは2つの朝廷（天皇）の戦い，この戦いに*巻き込まれて逃げまどう民衆の哀れな

146　Ⅶ. 日本歴史の旅

5. Establishment of Feudal Society

The Time Traveller is now moving on from the aristocratic society to the time of the feudal warriors.

In the second half of the Heian period, increases in agricultural production have led to the growth of powerful local warlords and the appearance of samurai warriors. In the beginning, these warriors who are mounted on horse back and armed with bows, arrows and swords fight each other to defend their land and expand their influence. As time passes they form feudal ties to the local warlords and grow from small bands into large armies.

Now we are in the middle of the eleventh century. As you can see, up in the northern regions of Honshu, many great battles are fought in rapid succession. The Minamoto clan emerges supreme from these wars and brings them to a conclusion. The Taira is another famous family of warriors who reached high social status in Kyoto formerly reserved for the aristocrats.

The year 1185 marks the end of the famous Gempei War at Dan-no-Ura. We are lucky to be able to watch this great naval battle. There are so many ships they are hard to count. In fact, there are 500 Taira ships and 840 Minamoto ships. At last, the Taira are annihilated by the Minamoto forces.

Here we are in yet another center of political power. This

姿が見えますか。家財を持ってうろうろする人たち、この時代に生まれなくて本当によかったですね。

　14世紀後半、様相はだいぶ違っています。権力の中心は新しい幕府のもとに京都に戻ります。もはや朝廷はほとんど力がなく、足利氏の室町幕府がただ一つの中央政権です。

　今までいろいろ恐ろしいことを見てきましたが、最悪の事態になりました。15世紀、京都の街が焼けています。皇居や公家、武家の家、寺社の建築や宝物まで。なんて惜しいことをするのでしょう。11年も続いた「応仁の乱」の結果です。タイムカプセルから飛び出して宝物を持ってきたいくらいですね。あれほど美しかった京都も今は焼け野原です。

　日本の各地ではこれから100年もの間、戦国時代が続きます。このころには手工業が各地に広まり、また各地に都市が作られていきます。農民たちは激しく変動する世の中で、村の*自治を行い、*一揆をおこして抵抗するまでに成長してきました。今までは*自給自足だった農民の生活も、定期的に市が開かれるようになり経済圏が広がっていきます。あちこちに活躍する商人たちの姿が見られますね。

　この時代の文化の*担い手たちは民衆です。猿楽能、狂言、おとぎぞうし（室町時代の短編物語）、これらは*民衆によって愛されたものです。

VOCABULARY　*Bakufu:* military government　*Buke seiji:* rule by warrior clans　*Tosotsu:* system of government　*Makikomareru:* be caught up in　*Jichi:* self-government　*Ikki:* uprising　*Jikyu jisoku:* self sufficient　*Ninau:* support　*Minshu:* ordinary people

is Kamakura in the year 1192, where Yoritomo, leader of the Minamoto clan, establishes his bakufu (military government) after that battle against the Taira we have just watched. This is the beginning of seven hundred years of rule by warrior clans continuing up to the end of the Edo period. Yoritomo carefully develops a system of government to control the warriors who were his retainers, but the political powers in Kyoto maintain their former strength.

We'll take the Time Traveller into the battles of this time. The Kamakura military government is overthrown by the samurais supporting the emperor. Next, on into the wars between the two courts with their rival emperors. Can you see the pitiful sight of the ordinary people caught up in these wars trying to flee? At least one good thing is that in these times there are no idle people around with fortunes to waste.

Things look a lot different in the second half of the fourteenth century. The political power has moved back to Kyoto, but now under a new bakufu. The Ashikaga military government of the Muromachi era is the sole central authority, while the court has almost no power at all.

We've seen some terrible things, but this may be the worst. It's the fifteenth century and Kyoto is burning. The palace and the mansions of the courtiers, temples and shrines and many treasures are all burned and destroyed. How on earth did such a terrible thing happen? This is the infamous Onin War that was fought out on the streets of Kyoto for eleven

6. 封建社会の完成

　戦国時代，日本の各地に戦国大名が生まれています。この中で諸大名の上に 統一政権を*樹立したのは，織田信長，豊臣秀吉，徳川家康の3人です。16世紀末までの織田，豊臣の時代を安土桃

long years. Don't you just want to jump out of the Time Traveller and rescue some of those treasures? Kyoto was so beautiful, and now it's just a burnt out ruin.

From this time on we have the Period of the Warring States that lasts for one hundred years. Handicrafts spread throughout Japan and towns are built all over the country. In this rapidly changing world, the farmers have a degree of self-government of their villages they never knew before. They grow in strength and confidence till they are able to mount uprisings against oppressive lords, and express their grievances in other ways too. The farmers were self-sufficient in their life styles before, but now they hold regular markets and economic units form in various parts of the country. Commerce begins to spread as independent tradesmen appear everywhere.

It is the ordinary people now who support the culture of this period. The Noh drama, the Kyogen comedies and the short stories of the Muromachi period reach heights of perfection. They are all forms of popular culture beloved by the ordinary people.

6. Consummation of Feudal Society

During the era of the Warring States the powerful warlords called daimyo emerge in various parts of Japan. The three most famous and powerful among them, Oda Nobunaga, Toyo-

山時代，徳川が封建時代の終わりまで*政権を握った17世紀以後を江戸時代といいます。

信長の安土城，秀吉の大坂城がここからもよく見えますね。大きな城，広くて深い堀，高く積みあげられた石垣，城の中心部には，天守閣が三層にも五層にも建てられ，君主の*威容を誇示しています。

この3人の時代には，いろいろな国々と国際貿易が行われ，古代の貴族文化とも，また*鎖国以後の江戸の町人文化とも異なる，力強い文化があります。社会は活気にあふれ民衆も平和な生活を楽しんでいます。このころの文化を桃山文化と呼びます。

江戸幕府の成立と鎖国

1600年，目の前で繰り広げられているのはあの有名な「関ケ原の戦い」です。豊臣氏をもり立てようとする諸大名と徳川家康の戦い，家康はこの戦いに勝って全国支配の実権を握るのです。豊臣秀吉は朝鮮に大軍を送ったが，家康は出兵もせず，実力を蓄えていた頭のよい家康，彼によってたてられた江戸幕府は彼の死後250年間も続くのです。

18世紀の初め，ここは江戸（今の東京）です。人口は100万人，ロンドンに並ぶ大都市です。

徳川氏は全国の大名たちを参勤交代¹などの厳しい制度で支配しています。また世襲的*身分制度によって，人々の生活は厳しく縛られています。武士（士）と農民（農）と町人（工・商）に分けられ，身分の違う人同士の間では，結婚することも難しいのです。

農民は全人口の80％を占めています。怠慢な武士の生活を支え

tomi Hideyoshi, and Tokugawa Ieyasu, gradually develop a unified administration for the government of the whole country. Oda and Toyotomi dominate the period up to the end of the sixteenth century, which is called the Azuchi-Momoyama period. The time from the beginning of the seventeenth when Tokugawa seized power up the end of feudalism is called the Edo period.

You should be able to see both Nobunaga's Azuchi Castle and Hideyoshi's Osaka Castle from here. They are enormous castles with wide, deep moats, and high stone walls. At the center of the castles are the towers rising to three and five stories, magnificent symbols of power of the lord.

Up to the time of these three great men, international trade was carried on and contacts were maintained with several countries. This vivid, vigorous culture was quite distinct from both the classical culture of the aristocrats that went before, and that of the merchant classes of the Edo period that came after the country was closed. Society flourished in many areas and the ordinary people enjoyed a peaceful way of life. This is called the Momoyama culture.

The Edo Bakufu and the Policy of National Isolation

The year is 1600 and what we see before us now is the famous battle of Sekigahara which pitted the daimyo, who supported Toyotomi, against Tokugawa Ieyasu. Ieyasu won this battle and went on to assume power over the whole coun-

ている彼らの生活は苦しそうですね。それに比べると町人たちの生活のなんと自由なこと！　農民のように重税を払う必要もなくもっとも安定した階層のようです。なぜでしょう。

　18世紀のこのころは*貨幣経済が 都市の生活ばかりでなく 農村にまで及んでいます。*年貢(ねんぐ)は米で 幕府に 納められますが，米を貨幣に換えるためには商人たちの手が必要だったからです。自給自足に近かった 農村の経済は 崩れ，封建社会の*基礎が揺らぎ始めています。

　年貢の重さに堪えられなくなった農民たちがあちこちで百姓(ひゃくしょう)一揆(いっき)を起こします。竹やりやかまを持って領主(りょうしゅ)の家を襲う農民たち，ものすごい勢いです。彼らも生きるために必死なのです。

　幕府の支配に 安定を取り戻そうと 何回かの 改革が 行われますが，もう幕府にその力はありません。19世紀，外国船が 日本の*沿岸に現れるようになります。

　少し周りの世界を見てみましょう。日本が鎖国を続けている間に，イギリス，フランス，アメリカなど欧米諸国は，インド，中国，東南アジアなどに進出し，民衆の抵抗を武力で抑えて，多くの*植民地を広げています。日本が鎖国政策をとらなかったら，どこかの国の植民地になっていたかもしれません。あなたはどう思いますか。

　資本主義の発達しつつある世界の中でもう日本は鎖国を続けているわけにはいきません。1853年アメリカの使節ペリーが黒ぬりの軍艦4隻を率いて浦賀に入港しています。人々の驚く様子を見てください。この人たちにとって煙突から煙を出す船など見るのは初めてなのですから。アメリカの強い開国の要求に，幕府はついに折れ自由貿易を行うことを認めます。これで日本の歴史にお

try. The wily Ieyasu had managed to avoid involvement in the Korean campaigns of Toyotomi Hideyoshi, and built up his power at home. The Edo bakufu he set up lasted for 250 years after his death.

Here we are in Edo at the beginning of the eighteenth century. Edo is now a great city with a population of a million people, almost as large as London in those days.

All daimyos are strictly subject to the Sankinkotai system by the Tokugawa regime. There are four social classes now: samurai, farmers, artisans and merchants, in that order of precedence. It is extremely difficult for members of different classes to intermarry.

About 80% of the total population are farmers. Supporting the lifestyles of the idle samurai, their life looks rather pitiful. In contrast, the life of the artisans and merchants looks pretty free. They do not have to pay the heavy taxes like the farmers, and they seem to have more security than the other classes. How did this come about?

In the eighteenth century the money economy has reached out from the towns into the rural villages. The bakufu collects the annual tax in rice, but only the merchants can convert the rice into money. This undermines the rural economy which had been close to self-sufficiency, and soon begins to shake the foundations of feudal society.

Here and there, the farmers who could not bear the heavy annual tax organize uprisings. They fight fiercely attacking the

いて200年あまりにわたる鎖国時代は終わります。

VOCABULARY　　*Juritsu suru:* develop (a unified administration)　*Seiken o nigiru:* seize power　　*Iyo:* magnificent symbols　　*Sakoku:* closed country (See p. 8)　　*Mibun seido:* social classes　　*Kahei keizai:* money economy　　*Nengu:* annual rice tax　　*Kiso ga yuragu:* shake the foundations　　*Engan:* coast　　*Shokuminchi:* colonies

注
1. 参勤交代
　　大名は1年おきに領地と江戸に住み，家族は江戸に住んだ。

houses of their lords with nothing but bamboo spears and sickles. It was a desperate but vain struggle for them.

Towards the end, the bakufu tries many reforms to bring back stability to its government, but it no longer has the power. For now we have reached the nineteenth century, and foreign ships appear off the coasts of Japan.

Let's take a look around the world at this time. While Japan maintained its seclusion policy, England, France and the other European and American powers have advanced into India, China and Southeast Asia, suppressing the peoples' resistance by force of arms, and establishing many colonies all over Asia. If Japan had not adopted its isolation policy, it too might have become a colony. What do you think?

Clearly, Japan could not continue in isolation from a world in which industrialism was rapidly advancing. In 1853 America sends its envoy, Captain Perry, with his four black ships into the Port of Uraga. Look at the surprised expressions on the faces of the people. This is the first time these people have seen smoke coming from the funnel of a ship. At length, bending to the strong demands from America to open the country, the bakufu recognizes free trade. This is the end of more than two hundred years of Japanese history under the policy of national isolation.

NOTES

1. This system involved feudal lords spending alternate years in the capital of Edo and on their own estates. Their families,

大名にとっては往復の費用，江戸での生活費など出費も多く苦しい政策だった。

7. 近代日本の成立

　黒船の恐怖と外国との貿易による物価の値上がりは，日本人の中にはじめて外国に対する日本という*国家意識を植えつけたかもしれません。今までの日本は無数の藩に*分割されていたので，外国に対する日本という意識は薄かったのです。

　1868年，260年も続いた江戸幕府が倒れ，天皇を中心とする*中央集権的な国家の基礎ができあがります。欧米の強国に対抗するためには幕府を倒して，統一国家を作るべきだという薩長同盟[1]が勝ったのです。

　*明治維新にはさまざまな改革が行われます。まず欧米文化をとり入れたこと。品川と横浜に汽車が走り始めた時の人々の驚く様子を見てください。これまで乗り物といえば，馬，かご，舟くらいだったのですから。なによりも*社会の仕組みが変わりました。士農工商という身分制度はなくなって，主権在民となり，かたちの上では身分の*不平等はなくなりました。そして農業が中心の社会は工業が中心の社会へと変わっていきます。

　1872年には小学校が義務教育になります。

　人々の服装を見てください。*ちょんまげを切って帽子をかぶるのが流行しています。着物を着て，靴をはいている人もずいぶんいますね。欧米の文化をとり入れた結果，人々の生活の仕方はこんなにも変わってきたのです。でも欧米文化の表面だけをまね

however, remained in Edo the whole time. Because of the heavy travelling and living expenses involved, this policy was extremely harsh.

7. Modern Japan

Commodity prices rise rapidly as trade with other countries begins. This, and the fear of the black ships, are perhaps the most important factors that first formed the national consciousness of the Japanese people. Before these dramatic changes, Japan was divided into countless daimyo estates, and there was only a vague awareness of foreign countries.

In 1868, after 260 years, the Edo bakufu falls, and the foundations for a national state based on the central power of the emperor are in place. The so-called Satcho League is victorious in the ensuing political struggles, with its plan to construct a unified national state capable of resisting the great powers of Europe and America.

A wide variety of reforms are brought about by the Meiji Restoration. The Japanese adopt Western culture with curiosity and enthusiasm. Just look at the expressions of disbelief on the faces of the people who see the first steam trains running between Shinagawa and Yokohama. Up to now the only kind of conveyances were horses, palanquins and boats. Indeed, the whole shape and appearance of society has changed. The four-class system is gone, and the doctrine of popular sovereignty

て，日本にある古くからの文化を軽視するのはちょっと困ったことですね。

政府は産業を盛んにするために欧米から機械を買い入れたり，兵器，火薬，造船などの*軍需工場を経営します。産業を盛んにして国を富ませ，強い軍隊を育てるためです。*富国強兵を方針とした政府は新しい軍隊を作るため，1873年に*徴兵令[2]を出します。徴兵制度によって，政府は庶民を*軍事訓練することができます。

そして1894年日清戦争が起こります。日本は隣の国，朝鮮の*支配権を得るために，中国と戦うことになるのです。日本はこの2つの国から文化や技術や思想を学んできました。江戸時代の鎖国政策の時代でさえ，中国とオランダの商船だけは，長崎に入ることができたというのに。

日本は半年あまりの戦争で清国に大勝利します。大喜びしている国民たち。日本はこの戦争で植民地（台湾）をもつ国となりました。このカプセルの中からでさえ，国民が軍国意識の中に巻き込まれていくのが分かりますね。

1904年，日露戦争，つまり日本とロシアの戦争が始まります。2つの国が韓国や中国東北部の支配権を争う戦争です。日本はこの戦争でも大勝利を収めます。しかし日本軍の*戦死者，33万9000人，夫や息子を失くした女性たち，父や兄弟を失った子供たちの悲しみ，気の毒で見ていられません。

日本は開国して半世紀しかたっていないというのに世界の強国の一つになりました。しかし国民の生活は苦しくなる一方で，はっきりと戦争に反対の立場をとる人も現れ始めました。しかし日本の*帝国主義化は進む一方です。

160　Ⅶ．日本歴史の旅

takes hold. Inequality of persons is formally abolished, and society's center of gravity shifts from agriculture to industry.

In 1872 compulsory education is instituted at the elementary school level.

Now look at the clothes the people are wearing. As you can see, it's popular among men to cut off their topknot or chonmage and wear a hat. There are lots of people in kimonos wearing Western-style shoes. This all amounts to a fundamental revolution for the entire population of Japan. But, clearly, it is not good enough just to copy the culture of the West and forget the long traditions of Japanese culture, don't you think?

The government is buying machines from the West to improve the output of industry and is running its own munitions factories to produce weapons and gunpowder as well as building warships. An efficient army and a prosperous country based on manufacturing are now primary national objectives in line with the new government's policy of "national prosperity and strong armed forces." Conscription is introduced in 1873 to achieve the latter goal. Conscription enabled the government to impose military training on the adult male population.

Japan goes to war with China in 1894, actually to secure control over its neighbor Korea. A great deal of culture, technology and philosophy and religion has come to Japan from both of these countries. Even under the closed country policy of the Edo period, ships from China and Holland, but only these countries, were allowed access to the port of Nagasaki

日露戦争で日本は朝鮮を植民地化します。朝鮮史を教えることを禁じたり，日本語を教えたりして，朝鮮人の民族としての自覚をなくして日本人に*同化させようとしたのです。

VOCABULARY　　*Kokka ishiki:* national consciousness　　***Bunkatsu suru:*** be divided　　*Chuoshuken:* central power　　*Meiji Ishin:* Meiji Restoration　　*Shakai no shikumi:* shape and appearance of society　　*Fubyodo:* inequality　　*Chonmage:* topknot　　*Gunju kojo:* munitions factories　　*Fukoku kyohei:* national prosperity and strong armed forces　　*Choheirei:* conscription　　***Gunji kunren:*** required to serve in the armed forces　　*Shihaiken:* secure control over　　*Senshisha:* war dead　　*Teikoku shugi ka:* advance of Japanese imperialism　　*Doka:* assimilation

in Kyushu.

After only six months, Japan wins a resounding victory over China which inspires the people with enthusiasm. This war also gives Japan a colony, Taiwan. Even from here in the Time Traveller, you can clearly see that there is a militarist atmosphere spreading among the people.

Here we are in 1904, and the war between Japan and Russia is about to begin. This war was fought over the issue of control of Korea and Northeast China. Another remarkable victory for Japan, but at the appalling cost of 339,000 Japanese dead. What a terrible sight to see the suffering of wives who lost husbands and sons, and children who lost fathers and brothers in this war.

Only half a century had elapsed since Japan opened the country, and already it has become a major world power. But the life of the common people has become very difficult, and for the first time in Japan there are people who campaign in opposition to war. On the other hand, of course, Japanese imperialism is advancing too.

Korea becomes a Japanese colony after the war with Russia. Forbidding the teaching of Korean history and forcing the Korean people to learn Japanese, all of these steps are aimed at destroying the Korean national consciousness and assimilating Koreans as Japanese.

注

1. 薩長同盟
   国の統一のために，九州の薩摩藩と長州藩は同盟を結び，徳川幕府討幕のために戦った。
2. 徴兵令
   国民の男子に兵役の義務を課した（20歳以上の男子に3年間）。これによって日本に常備軍が生まれた（35000人）。

8. 二度の世界大戦

19世紀の末です。欧米の帝国主義諸国は，植民地や勢力範囲をめぐる争いを背景に，産業を盛んにし，*軍備の*拡充を続けています。こうした対立がやがて，世界を戦争へともっていきます。1914年，第一次世界大戦ぼっ発，オーストリア，ロシア，フランス，日本と参戦国は30か国にも上っています。歴史上初めての世界大戦です。ヨーロッパを主な戦場とするこの戦争で，ヨーロッパの各国は世界の市場から退き，逆に戦場から遠い日本とアメリカは，海上に市場を伸ばすことになります。

第一次大戦の結果，日本は*好景気を迎えます。*集中的な工業地帯が東京，大阪，北九州などにできています。ここから大阪を見てみましょう。大工場の煙突から出る黒い煙は労働者の住宅の低い屋根より高くのぼり，好景気とはいっても物価が上がったため人々の生活は苦しそうです。

そして第二次世界大戦，日本，ドイツ，イタリアはアメリカ，イギリスなど*連合国を相手に戦い，日本軍は半年後どんどん負

NOTES
1. Satcho League: The great daimyo estates of Satsuma and Choshu in Kyushu joined together and formed a league to overthrow the Tokugawa bakufu and unify the country under the Emperor.
2. All Japanese men over the age of twenty were required to serve in the armed forces for three years. This established a standing army of 35,000 men.

8. The Two World Wars

We have now arrived at the end of the nineteenth century. Against the backdrop of the power struggles over colonies and spheres of influence, industry in the imperialist countries of Europe and America is flourishing and their armies continue to expand. In 1914, we can see the start of the First World War in which a total of no less than thirty countries participated including Austria, Russia, France and Japan. This is the First World War in history. Europe is the main battleground, so many of the European countries have to withdraw from world markets, while Japan and America, far from the war fronts, expand their markets overseas.

Japan enters a phase of relative prosperity after the First World War. Tokyo, Osaka and Kyushu are among the main areas of concentration of industry. Let's take a look at Osaka from here. Black smoke is billowing into the sky from the

け始めていきます。しかしこのニュースは国民には伝えられません。このひどい状態，食べるものもなく，学生までが戦場に送られ，中学生や女学生は*軍需工場で働かされています。こんな状態がいつまで続くのでしょうか。

1945年8月，目の前に広がるきのこ雲，世界最初の原子爆弾が広島に落とされたのです。そのあと長崎にも落とされました。こんなことが歴史上あってはならなかった。これから先にも。

VOCABULARY　*Gunbi:* armies　*Kakuju:* expand　*Kokeiki:* prosperity　*Shuchuteki na kogyo chitai:* areas of concentration of industry　*Rengokoku:* allied powers

9. 新しい日本

1945年，*敗戦。日本の主な都市は*焼け野原になってしまいました。しかしわずか10年のうちに，日本の経済は戦前の*水準を追い抜き，1960年代には経済の*高度成長を遂げます。この高度成長につれて，日本人の大移動が始まっています。1966年，日本の人口は1億人を超えましたが，なかでも東京，大阪，名古屋な

smokestacks of the big factories, high above the low roofs of
the workers' houses. Now, even though the economy is good,
prices are rising and the life of the ordinary people still
looks grim.

Next, on to the Second World War. Japan, Germany and
Italy fight against the Allied powers centered around America
and Britain. After about the first six months, the Japanese
army begins to suffer defeats, but this news is withheld from
the people. Life deteriorates to dreadful levels during the war,
with no food to eat, students being sent to the war, and boys
and girls being forced to work in the munitions factories. How
long can this situation last?

August 1945. There it is. The mushroom cloud spreading
out in the sky before your very eyes. The world's first atom
bomb has been dropped on Hiroshima, and another will soon
be dropped on Nagasaki. History should never have seen this.
The future should not, either.

9. The New Japan

After the defeat of 1945, the major cities of Japan are now
nothing but charred and burnt out ruins. But look, within
the short space of just ten years, the Japanese economy over-
takes the prewar economy, and in the 1960's it enters a period
of high economic growth, and with it the great migrations of

どへの人口の集中が目立ちます。このころから日本の*商社マンが世界、とくに東南アジアの各地で走りまわっています。

　日本は*経済大国として成長しました。1970年代、*公害の問題が表面化します。高度成長の*ツケが回ってきたのです。

　1980年代、日本の商品は世界の市場にはん濫しています。*円高傾向が続き、*倒産する会社もでてきました。日本が世界から信頼されてゆくためには、*民主主義を守り育てていくことです。二度と戦争の時代が来ることのないように！

　皆さん、タイムカプセル歴史の旅はいかがでしたか？　日本の歴史の流れがお分かりいただけたでしょうか。なにぶん限られた時間ですので、細かいところまでお見せできなかったのが残念です。ともかく旅を楽しんでいただけましたか？

　今度は21世紀からの未来への旅に皆さんをご案内しましょう。その旅が楽しいものであることを願っています。

　では皆さん、さようなら。

VOCABULARY　　*Haisen:* defeat　*Yakenohara:* charred and burnt out ruins　*Suijun:* levels　*Kodo seicho:* high economic growth　*Shosha man:* trading companies　*Keizai taikoku:* great economic power　*Kogai:* pollution　*Tsuke ga mawaru:* reckon　*Endaka keiko:* rise in value of the yen　*Tosan suru:* go bankrupt　*Minshushugi:* democracy

the Japanese people begin. In 1966 the Japanese population exceeds one hundred million, but there are massive concentrations of people in the big cities like Tokyo, Osaka and Nagoya. From this period on Japanese trading companies begin to advance into countries all around the world, particularly in Southeast Asia.

Japan has grown into a great economic power. Pollution has become a prominent problem in the 1970's; surely a kind of reckoning for the high growth rates.

In the 1980's Japanese goods are inundating markets everywhere. The value of the yen continues to rise and many companies go bankrupt. Japan is very careful to develop democracy in the country, among other reasons to win the trust and friendship of the rest of the world. And let's hope that the country never goes to war again.

So how was the trip through Japanese history in the Time Traveller? I hope you were able to get a sense of the flow of Japanese history, even though we did not have more than a few minutes. It's a shame we were not able to go into greater detail at some of those places. At any rate, I hope you enjoyed it.

Perhaps next time we can take a trip into the future, into the 21st century. It should be enjoyable.

Well everybody, sayonara!

Ⅷ. 日本の文学 (時代の背景)

1. 万葉集

　日本に，大和地方を中心とする古代国家が誕生したのは4世紀の後半です。このころから，中国文化の影響を受け，漢字[1]を用いて歌が書かれるようになりました。

　『万葉集』はこのような時代に成立したものです。*作者層は，天皇，皇族から広く庶民にまで及んでいて，歌の数は4500首にもなります。各作品の年代は4世紀ごろから8世紀後半までの450年もの長期間にわたっています。

　　万葉集の*部立
　　　「相聞歌」（主として恋の歌）
　　　「挽歌」　（主として死を悼む歌）
　　　「雑歌」　（種々の歌）

　これほどの長い期間，これほど広い階層の人々の作品を集めた歌集は，ほかには存在しないでしょう。また，『万葉集』は*支配者側からの*視点で作品が選ばれたわけではないので，人々のさまざまな生活を，いろいろな角度からみることができます。

　*歌風は時代によって少しずつ異なりますが，感じたまま，見

VIII. Aspects of Japanese Literature

1. Manyoshu (The Collection of Ten Thousand Leaves)

With the Yamato region of the country for its centre, Japan as an ancient state came into existence during the latter half of the fourth century A.D. From that time onwards, under the influence of Chinese civilisation, the writing of poetry became possible through the use of Chinese characters.

It was at such a time that *The Manyoshu* ("Collection of Ten Thousand Leaves") anthology of poems was compiled. The poets included range from emperors and members of the aristocracy to ordinary citizens and the number of poems comes to as many as four thousand five hundred. Individual poems were written at different times over a long period of four hundred and fifty years from the fourth century A.D. to the second half of the eighth.

The arrangement of the poems in *The Manyoshu* is as follows:

1. Somonka (Poems chiefly about love)
2. Banka (Elegies and dirges, principally lamentations on death)

たままを，*直感的に 5・7調[2]でうたっているといえるでしょう。

　君待つとあが恋<ruby>ひ<rt>こ</rt></ruby>をれ ばわが宿の
　　*すだれ動かし秋の風吹く　　　　<ruby>額田王<rt>ぬかたのおおきみ</rt></ruby>

（あなたをお待ちして私が恋しく思っていると，私の家のすだれを動かして秋の風が吹いてきます。）

VOCABULARY　　*Sakushaso:* poets included　　*Budate:* organisation, arrangement　　*Shihaisha:* rulers　　*Shiten:* point of view　　*Kafu:* poetic style　　*Chokkanteki:* intuitively　　*Sudare:* bamboo blinds

---
注

1. 漢字
『万葉集』が記録されたころはまだ仮名がなかった。そのために漢字だけを用いて書かれている。漢字をどのように読むべきかという規則はないので，今日でも意味のわからない歌がいくつかある。
2. 5・7調
和歌や詩の音数律の一つで，5音句，7音句の順に繰り返す。

3. Zoka (Miscellaneous poems)

There is probably no other collection of poetry in existence that was compiled over such a long period and that includes the works of poets from such a broad segment of society. In addition, since the poems in *the Manyoshu* were not selected from the exclusive point of view of the ruling classes, we can see vividly reflected in them, human society as it really was.

The poetic style varies somewhat according to the period but, in lines of five and seven syllables, they all express how people felt and what they saw.

Here is an example, by Nukada no Okimi.

Kimi matsu to	As I wait for you,
Aga koi oreba	I am filled with longing
Waga yado no	The autumn wind blows
Sudare ugokashi	Swaying the bamboo screens
Aki no kaze fuku	of my house.

NOTES

1. When *the Manyoshu* was compiled, the native kana system of writing did not exist. For that reason, only Chinese characters were used to write the poems. As there are no rules governing the deciphering of Chinese characters, there are still many poems whose meanings are not understood.
2. One system of meter in waka poems consisting of successive lines of five and seven syllables.

2. 枕草子(まくらのそうし)

『源氏物語』が書かれ始めるわずか前の1000年前後、清少納言(せいしょうなごん)[1]によって、新しい文学形式である随筆『枕草子』が書かれました。

紫式部が宮廷生活を写実的に描いたのに対して、清少納言は心に感じたことを豊かな*感受性で描いています。*簡潔で*独創的な鋭い文体は*批評的であり、時には*哲学的でさえあります。

当時、公私の記録は漢文体で書かれていましたが、自分の感情を記録するには*不向きだったようです。そこで仮名文の発達につれて、文学的価値の高い日記・随筆などが女性たちによって書かれ、多くの平安女流文学者たちが*出現しました。清少納言はその中でも、もっとも個性的で、自由に自分の*見聞や体験を書いた女性といえるでしょう。

『枕草子』は長短約300段から成り、次の諸段に分けられます。

1. 類集的諸段[2]
2. 随想的諸段[3]
3. 日記的諸段[4]

VOCABULARY *Kanjusei:* sensitivity, susceptibility *Kanketsu:* terse, laconic *Dokusoteki:* original *Hihyoteki:* critical *Tetsugakuteki:* philosophical *Fumuki:* unsuitable, unfit for *Shutsugen suru:* realise *Kenbun:* observation

注――――――――――――――――――
1. 清少納言 (965—1025)

2. Makura no Soshi (The Pillow Book)

About the year 1000, only a short time before *Genji Monogatari* was written, Sei Shonagon composed *Makura no Soshi* ("Pillow Book") in a new literary form, the Zuihitsu (Random Jottings).

In contrast to Murasaki Shikibu's realistic depiction of life at court, Sei Shonagon describes with deep sensitivity her innermost emotions. At the same time, however, she writes in a laconic and original style that can be critical and even philosophical.

At that time official documents, both public and private, were written in Chinese style. However, this was unsuitable for recording one's own private feelings. Accordingly, with the development of the native kana script, diaries and occasional writings of high literary quality were written by women and many female literary figures appeared in the Heian Period. Amongst these, Sei Shonagon was the freest and most individual when it came to writing down her own observations and experiences.

Makura no Soshi is made up of three hundred shorter or longer sections comprising three main groups, viz. 1. Comparisons and analogies. 2. Random thoughts. 3. Diary entries.

NOTES
1. *Sei Shonagon* (965–1025): She served as a maid-in-waiting

一条天皇の皇后定子に仕えた。
 2. 類集的諸段
　　「木の花は」「鳥は」のように美的連想を語るもの。
 3. 随想的諸段
　　自然や人事の世界を描く。
 4. 日記的諸段
　　作者の10年にわたる宮仕え生活を描いたもの。

3.　源氏物語

　平安時代の*宮廷貴族の生活を想像する時，私たちの頭の中にまず浮かぶのは，『源氏物語』の世界ではないでしょうか。
　作者は紫式部¹，物語は54*帖からなっています。各帖には物語の世界を*暗示するような「桐壺」²「夕顔」³ などという名前がつけられています。物語は「光源氏」⁴ の誕生，愛の*遍歴，*出家を願う姿，死，主人公の死後残された人々の世界が，*雄大な構想の中に語られています。

　世界最古の長編小説としても*名高く，*陰影に富んだ美しい文体，*巧みに配された和歌，そして人物の性格や心理描写など，『源氏物語』は中世から近代の作家に大きな影響を与えてきました。

　この物語の主題が何であるかは，読む人によって違ってくるでしょう。しかし時代も環境もまったく違う10世紀の貴族社会の物語に，私たちがこれほど胸を打たれるのは，全体に流れる「もののあわれ⁵」のせいではないでしょうか。

to the wife of the Emperor Ichijo.
2. *Ruishuteki*: Comparisons are made through a beautiful association of ideas in such sections beginning "Flowering trees are...", "Birds are...", etc.
3. *Zuisoteki* (Random Thoughts): Descriptions of nature and the world of men.
4. *Nikkiteki* (Diary Entries): Records of the author's ten years as a court maid-in-waiting.

3. Genji Monogatari (The Tale of Genji)

When we try to imagine the life of court nobility during the Heian Period, it is surely the world of *Genji Monogatari* ("The Tale of Genji") that comes to mind.

The writer was Murasaki Shikibu and the story is made up of fifty-four chapters. Each one has such names as Kiritsubo or Yugao, etc. for a title and these hint at kind of world described in the tale. Conceived on a grand scale, the story deals with the world of Hikaru no Genji ("Shining Genji"), his birth, his life and loves, his entry into the priesthood and death and of the people who survived him.

Genji Monogatari is highly regarded as the oldest novel in the world. With its beautiful, richly nuanced style, into which waka poetry has been skilfully incorporated, and psychological description of people's characters, it has exerted a tremendous influence on Japanese writers from the middle ages to the

VOCABULARY　　*Kyutei kizoku:* nobility or court nobility　*Joo:* chapter　　*Anji suru:* hint at　　*Henreki:* record　　***Shukke (suru)*** : enter the priesthood　　*Yudai:* grand　　*Nadakai:* of high regard　　*In'ei:* nuance　　*Takumi:* skilfully

注
1. 紫式部 (978—1016)
   父は詩人漢文学者として名高い。夫に死別後,『源氏物語』を書き始め,一条天皇の中宮彰子に仕えた。
2. 桐壷
   第1巻,源氏誕生から12歳まで。
3. 夕顔
   第4巻,夕顔という娘との出会い。
4. 光源氏
   物語の主人公。
5. もののあわれ
   人の心がある対象に触れた時にわき出る自然的感動。

4. 平家物語

　平安末期から12世紀後半の鎌倉期にかけて,多くの武士たちによる*戦乱がありました。『平家物語』は平家一門の全盛と滅亡[1]を*主題とした,軍記物語[2]の*代表作です。文章は雅語[3],俗語[4],仏語[5],漢語[6]などを*自在に取り入れた和漢混交文[7]で,全体に仏

present day.

What the novel's principal theme is will vary according to the reader. But what moves us the most, surely in *Genji Monogatari*, with its description of the totally different epoch and circumstances of aristocratic society in the tenth century, is the sense of "mono no aware" (awareness of the pathos of things") that runs through it all.

NOTES
1. *Murasaki Shikibu* (978–1016): Her father was a famous poet and scholar of Chinese literature. After the death of her husband she began to write *Genji Monogatari* and became a maid of honour to the Emperor Ichijo.
2. *Kiritsubo*: The title of Chapter 1. It deals with the life of Genji to the age of twelve.
3. *Yugao*: Chapter 4. It is about Genji's meeting with the girl, Yugao.
4. *Hikaru Genji*: "Shining Genji" the hero of the story.
5. *Mono no aware*: The pathos or pity of things.

4. Heike Monogatari (The Tale of the Heike)

From the end of the Heian Period to the Kamakura Period, wars took place involving most members of the military class. These wars are the theme of *Heike Monogatari* ("The Tale of the Heike") which tells of the rise and fall of the Heike

教思想が流れています。

　成立した年代も作者もはっきりとは分かっていません。琵琶法師という*盲目の芸人が，琵琶を*伴奏にして『平家物語』を語り広めていく中で，多くの作者たちによって物語は*統一されていったと思えます。ある時は勇壮に，またある時は悲壮に，平家一門が*繁栄し，やがて西海に*滅び去ってゆく様子を物語る琵琶法師，多くの民衆がこの物語に涙を流したことでしょう。

　日本人には昔から判官びいき[3]と言って，弱者の立場にあるものに，同情する気持ちが強いようです。

VOCABULARY　*Senran:* battle, war　　*Shudai:* theme, motif　*Daihyosaku:* representative work　　*Jizai:* free, unrestricted　　*Momoku:* blind　　*Banso:* accompaniment　　*Toitsu:* unification, unity　*Han'ei:* prosperity　　*Horobisaru:* be destrored and vanish

---
注
1. 平家一門の全盛と滅亡
　　貴族社会を破った平家が繁栄し，滅びるまでの約20年。
2. 軍記物語
　　歴史的な事実に基づいて，合戦を素材とした文学。
3. 雅語
　　詩歌，古文の表現に使われたことば。
4. 俗語

clan in what is the representative example of the Gunki (Military Epic) genre of literature. Imbued throughout with Buddhist philosophy, the book is written in a mixed Sino-Japanese style (*wakan konkobun*). The book contains language used by the aristocracy (*gago*), the common people (*zokugo*), Buddhist priests (*butsugo*), as well as Chinese expressions (*kango*).

The date of composition and the writer of *Heike Monogatari* are unknown. But, with the growth in the number of minstrels, who were blind, itinerant priests reciting stories about the Heike to the accompaniment of the biwa (Japanese lute), it is thought to be the combined result of many hands. Doubtless many tears flowed as the common people listened to the sometimes heroic, sometimes tragic tale, as told by the minstrels, of the rise to power and glory of the Heike clan before its destruction beneath the waves of the western sea.

From ancient times, the Japanese have shown great sympathy for those in a weak position or on the losing side and this feeling is expressed in the expression Hoganbiiki ("favouring the underdog").

NOTES

1. After their overthrow of the aristocracy, the period of the prosperity of the Heike to their downfall was approximately twenty years.
2. *Gunki Monogatari*: Military epics based on historical events.
3. *Gago*: Words and expressions used in poetry and ancient literature.
4. *Zokugo*: Language of everyday life.

日常の社会生活に普通に使われることば。
 5. 仏語
　　　仏教に使われることば。
 6. 漢語
　　　日本人に古くから使われた中国語。
 7. 和漢混交文
　　　漢字，かなで書かれた文。
 8. 判官びいき
　　　兄にしっとされて滅びた，源義経に対する同情の気持ち。

5.　日本永代蔵

「人の家にあった方がいいものは，梅，桜，松，楓などと言われているが，そんなものよりもっと大切なのは，金銀米銭です」(口語訳)……井原西鶴（1642—93）によって書かれた『日本永代蔵』はこんなふうに始まります。

　江戸時代，*商工業が発達し，各種の*庶民文学が起こりました。それは京都，大阪を中心としたものであり，上方文化とも言われています。これは西鶴に始まる浮世草子¹，近松門左衛門(1653—1724) の浄瑠璃²が主なものです。

　西鶴は江戸時代の人々の生活を*現実的に描きました。その内容から好色物³，武家物⁴，町人物⁵，説話物⁶に分けることができます。

　『日本永代蔵』は町人が金持ちになった話を主とする30話からなっていて，金を中心とした*町人社会の有様が，実に生き生きと描かれています。そのころ使われていた言葉を，文章の中に使

5. *Butsugo*: Language of Buddhism.
6. *Kango*: The Chinese language as used by the Japanese since olden times.
7. *Wakan Konkobun*: Literature involving the use of both Chinese characters and Japanese native kana.
8. *Hoganbiiki*: Sympathy felt by the Japanese for Minamoto no Yoshitsune who was destroyed by the jealously of his elder brother.

5. Nihon Eitai Gura (The Japanese Family Storehouse)

Written by Ihara Saikaku, *Nihon Eitai Gura* ("The Japanese Family Storehouse") begins in this way. "People's houses are said to need plum, cherry, pine and maple trees. But far more important than things such as that are gold, silver, rice and copper coins."

With the development of the trade and industry, a variety of popular literature came into existence during the Edo Period. This phenomenon was concentrated mainly in the Kyoto-Osaka region. It is known as the Kamigata culture. The best examples can be found in the Ukiyozoshi of Saikaku and the Joruri (puppet dramas) of Chikamatsu Monzaemon.

Saikaku's realistic descriptions of people's lives in the Edo Period can be divided into the following categories: Koshokumono, Bukemono, Choninmono and Setsuwamono.

ったことが、文章を面白くした原因の一つかもしれません。

VOCABULARY　　*Shokogyo:* trade and industry　　*Shomin bungaku:* popular (lowbrow) literature　　*Genjitsuteki:* realistic　　*Chonin shakai:* urban mercantile society

注
1. 浮世草子
   元禄時代 (1688—1704) を主として、その前後約90年間、上方を中心に行われた現実主義的な小説。
2. 浄瑠璃
   三味線に合わせて語る語りもの。人形浄瑠璃は物語、人形、三味線が一体になったもの。
3. 好色物
   男女の愛欲の世界を描いたもの。
4. 武家物
   義理に生きる当時の武士の生活を描いたもの。
5. 町人物
   町人生活の実態を描いたもの。
6. 説話物
   作者が諸国を旅行して見聞した話など。

6. 奥の細道

「月日は百代の過客にして、行きかふ年も又旅人なり」(月日は*永遠に旅を続けて行くものであり、来ては去り、去っては来る

Nihon Eitai Gura is made up of 30 stories mainly about people who succeed in becoming rich. That they constitute such lively descriptions of urban, mercantile society, where money was the main preoccupation, may be due in part to the introduction of colloquial language used at the time thus making for a more interesting style.

NOTES
1. Realistic novels that were written for about ninety years in the Kamigata (Kyoto-Osaka) region starting from the Genroku Period (1688–1704).
2. Narration performed to shamisen accompaniment. In Ningyo Joruri the narrated story, puppets and shamisen function together as a single entity.
3. Novels about the relations between the sexes.
4. Novels describing the lives, motivated by honour and duty, of warriors of the time.
5. Novels describing the actual conditions of mercantile life in the cities.
6. Novels based on what the author has heard and seen in his travels around the country.

6. Oku no Hosomichi (The Narrow Road to the Distant North)

"The days and months are travellers of eternity. So are the passing years".

年々も，また旅人です。)

　作者の松尾芭蕉¹の*生涯は旅と俳諧です。芭蕉の詩心は旅によって育てられ，旅によって*磨かれたのではないでしょうか。今は東北新幹線で3時間半もあれば岩手県まで行ってしまいます。しかし当時は乗り物と言っても*かごか舟くらいしかなく，芭蕉はこの旅に7か月を要しています。

　『奥の細道』には芭蕉が東北各地を旅行した時の*風物，*人情などが簡潔な文章によって書かれていて，*紀行文の*典型と言われています。文中には51句の俳句²がはさまれています。

　ほんの数日間で東北を一周できるような現代に芭蕉が生きていたとしたら，こんなすばらしい紀行文は生まれなかったでしょう。

VOCABULARY　*Eien:* eternity, immortality　*Shogai:* life, career　*Migakareru:* be polished, perfected　*Kago:* palanquin　*Fubutsu:* scenery　*Ninjo:* customs and manners　*Kikobun:* travelogue　*Tenkei:* model, pattern, ideal

注―――――――――――――――――――――――――――
1. 松尾芭蕉（1644—1694）
　通俗的であった俳諧を新しい芸術として創りあげた。
2. 俳句
　5音，7音，5音の17音で構成された短詩。

7. 夏目漱石（坊ちゃん）

　『坊ちゃん』を読み始めると，その*そう快なリズムが快く，つ

The life of the poet Matsuo Basho was made up of travel and haikai. It can even be said that his poetic gift was cultivated and perfected by travel. Nowadays it is possible to reach Iwate Prefecture in three hours and half by means of the Bullet Train. In Basho's day, the only vehicles were palanquins and ships and, to make the same journey, he needed seven months.

Oku no Hosomichi is the record of Basho's journey through the northern Tohoku district. It is reckoned to be a model of the travelogue literary genre for its terse descriptions of scenery, customs and manners. Also included in the text are fifty-one haiku poems.

If Basho had lived in the present day when it is possible to see the Tohoku region in a few days, this superb travelogue would surely not have come into existence.

NOTES
1. *Matsuo Basho* (1644–1694): It was he who transformed the hitherto popular pastime of haikai composition into a new art form.
2. *Haiku*: The first stanza of a haikai poem consisting of 17 syllables, three lines of 5, 7 and 5.

7. Natsume Soseki (Botchan)

Once you begin to read *Botchan* its exhilarating rhythm is

い*一気に読み終えてしまう。文章は*平明で分かりやすく、坊ちゃんの性格は*正義感が強く、いくらか*軽率でもある。

作者の夏目漱石が一年の間に体験した中学校での教師生活が、この小説のモデルになっていると思うが、田舎に来た都会の青年のとまどいといらだちが*随所に顔を出し面白い。「なんだか生徒全体がおれひとりを*探偵しているように思われた。」と彼が言うように、てんぷらそばを4杯食べたとか、湯の中で泳いだとか、あちこちで坊ちゃんは見張られている。

明治初年、舞台は*田舎の*城下町、江戸っ子の見た田舎の*人情風俗をとおして、坊ちゃん(漱石)の社会、風俗への*批判精神が興味深い。彼は日本人の好む*典型的な性格だろう。

夏目漱石(1867—1916)は、英文学専攻の学者として出発したが、1905年『吾輩は猫である』で文名があがる。他に『草枕』『三四郎』『それから』『門』『こころ』など。

VOCABULARY *Sokai:* refreshing, exhilarating, stimulating
Ikki: in one go, at a single sitting   *Heimei:* plain, clear, simple
Seigikan: sense of justice, right and wrong   *Keisotsu:* rash, hasty
Zuisho: everywhere   *Tantei suru:* spy on, investigate   *Inaka:* country, rural   *Jokamachi:* castle town   *Ninjofuzoku:* customs and manners   *Hihan:* criticism, comment   *Tenkeiteki:* typical

so agreeable that you find you have finished the book in a single sitting. The writing is clear and easy to understand and the personality of Botchan, himself, has a strong sense of right and wrong even if he is a trifle hasty.

The novel, I think is based upon the author, Natsume Soseki's one year of experience as a teacher at a middle school. But its interest lies in the way the confusions and frustrations of city-raised boy, newly arrived in the country, keep cropping up at every turn. "I felt that all the other children in the school were spying on my every move". As Botchan, himself, says he is constantly watched for the antics to like devouring four bowlsful of tempura noodles or swimming about in the communal bathtub.

The story is set in a provincial castle town in the late 1860's. "For its description of rural life and manners seen through the eyes of a boy born and raised in the capital of Edo, Botchan is of the greatest interest as an expression of Soseki's views and criticisms of society and customs at that time". Botchan's character is of a type much liked by the Japanese.

Natsume Soseki (1867–1916) started out as a scholar of English literature but, in 1905, he made a name for himself as a writer with *Wagahai wa Neko de aru* ("I am a Cat"). His other works include *Kusamakura* ("Pillow of Grass"), *Sanshiro, Sorekara* ("And Then"), *Mon* ("Gate"), *Kokoro* ("Heart"), etc.

8. 芥川竜之介

　芥川竜之介（1892—1927）は大正期¹の代表的な短編小説家です。1916年，24歳の時「鼻」を夏目漱石に認められ，*文壇に華々しく登場した。材料として「鼻」を採り上げたことが新しいだけでなく，不思議なユーモアがある。このあと，彼は次々と短編を発表する。「羅生門」，「芋粥」，「蜘蛛の糸」，「トロッコ」，「河童」，どの作品も一語一句が*選び抜かれたもので，何回読み返してみても感心するばかりだ。

　第一高等学校時代には英・仏・独・露などの文学作品を原書や英訳で*手当たりしだい読んだことが，彼の級友にあてた手紙から分かる。彼の作風にアナトール・フランスなどの外国作家の影響がみられるのは，そのためだろう。森鷗外（1862—1922）の歴史小説や夏目漱石からの*感化も強いといわれる。しかし彼は『今昔物語』²やキリシタン文学など*未開拓の分野から素材を発見し，芥川独自の分野を作りあげた。

　*私小説化，プロレタリア化するそのころの文壇で，ひとり，若さに満ちた制作を続けていた芥川も，胃を病み，神経を病み，「ぼんやりした不安」（*遺書）から，自殺してしまう。

　私達の前にいる彼は，いつまでも35歳の若さである。彼が望んだ「最高の静けさ」の中で……。

VOCABULARY　　*Bundan:* literary scene　　*Erabinukareru:* be selected　　*Teatarishidai:* at random, anything one can lay one's hands on　　*Kanka:* influence　　*Mikaitaku:* uncultivated, unexplored　　*Shishosetsu:* "I" novels　　*Isho:* suicide note

8. Akutagawa Ryunosuke

Akutagawa Ryunosuke (1892–1927) is the representative short story writer of the Taisho Period. He made a brilliant entry onto the literary scene in 1916 with his *Hana* ("Nose") which was praised by Natsume Soseki and which was new not only for its subject but also for its unusual humour. Akutagawa went on subsequently to publish one story after the other, *Rashomon, Imogayu, Kumo no Ito, Torokko, Kappa,* etc. Every word of which has been so carefully chosen that one is always impressed even with repeated reading.

From letters that he sent to his classmates we know that, while a student at First High School he read anything he could lay his hands on by European writers (English, French, German, Russian, etc.) either in the original languages or in English translations. It is for that reason no doubt that the influence of foreign writers like Anatole France can be seen in his style. It can also be said that the influence of the historical novels of Mori Ogai is very strong, as well as that of Natsume Soseki. But he also drew inspiration from such unexplored areas as the world of the *Konjaku Monogatari* and Japanese Christian literature to cultivate his own distinctive field.

At a time when the Japanese literary scene was dominated by autobiographical novels told in the first person ("I" novels) and proletarian writings, Akutagawa continued, independently,

注
1. 大正期
   (1912—1926年)。
2. 『今昔物語』
   日本最大の古説話集で、12世紀初めの成立。1200余の説話が収められている。

9. 川端康成（雪国）

　川端康成は両親が幼くして亡くなったため、祖父母に育てられるが、その祖父母とも16歳で*死別し、*孤児となった。もし私たちが川端の作品の中に流れる感情の本体を捜そうとするなら、この辺が*原点ではないだろうか。つまり自分は寒いところにいながら、暖かいものを得たいと願っている……。

「国境の長いトンネルを抜けると雪国であった」

『雪国』の有名な書き出しである。これは川端の戦前の代表作で、近代日本*抒情小説の古典ともいえる。

creating works in which his youthful vigour was clearly manifest. But he began to suffer physically from stomach problems, as well as psychologically and, after complaining in the suicide note (isho) that he left behind, of "a vague unrest", he killed himself.

Having reached the "deepest silence" that he longed for Akutagawa always remains before us a youthful thirty-five.

NOTES

1. Taisho Period (1912–1926).
2. *Konjaku Monogatari* (Tales of Past and Present): Japan's largest collection of ancient tales. It was compiled in the twelfth century and contains approximately 1,200 stories.

9. Kawabata Yasunari (Yuki Guni)

As his parents died when he was still a child, Kawabata Yasunari was brought up by his grandfather and grandmother. They also died when he was sixteen years of age leaving him an orphan. It is surely in this area that we must look if we wish to discover the source of the feeling that flows through Kawabata's works. In other words, from his position in the cold, he constantly longs for warmth.

> "Emerging from the tunnel connecting the two regions, the train entered the snow country."

雪におおわれた山や風俗，習慣の違った地方に滞在し，そこで主人公の島村は2人の女性，駒子(こまこ)，葉子(ようこ)に出会う。駒子，命をかけて男を愛している女，「精いっぱいに生きている」女，私たちはいつのまにか川端を島村に置き換えて駒子を見詰める。雪国という舞台背景と，そこに生きる2人の女。

　日本では何回も映画化され，舞台化された。この作品には川端の世界が*凝縮されている。

　川端康成（1899—1972）の代表作は『伊豆の踊子』『雪国』『千羽鶴』『山の音』である。1968年，ノーベル文学賞を受けた。1972年，自殺。

VOCABULARY　*Shibetsu suru*: die, pass away　　*Koji*: orphan
Genten: source　　*Jojo shosetsu*: lyrical novel　　*Gyoshuku suru (sareru)*: condense, be condensed

10. 谷崎潤一郎（春琴抄(しゅんきんしょう)）

　谷崎潤一郎の作品には女性*崇拝の主張が多くみられる。中でも『痴人(ちじん)の愛』にみられるような，男性の*官能的欲望から生ま

This is the famous opening line of *Yukiguni* ("Snow Country"), Kawabata's most important pre-war work and one which can be said to be a classic of the contemporary Japanese lyrical novel.

Amid the snow covered mountains and buildings of a distant region that has its own customs and manners, the hero, Shimamura, discovers two women: Komako and Yoko. And Komako, in particular, is a woman who, when she loves a man, does so with her whole being. "She lives with all her might". Before we realise it, we find ourselves substituting Kawabata for Shimamura and gazing at Komako through his eyes. It is the story of two women who exist against the background of the snow country.

Kawabata's whole "world" has been contained within this novel, one which has been staged and filmed many times.

Kawabata Yasunari's principal works are *Izu no Odoriko* ("The Izu Dancer"), *Yukiguni* ("Snow Country"), *Senbazuru* "A Thousand Cranes", *Yama no Oto* ("The Sound of the Mountain"). He was awarded the Nobel Prize for Literature in 1968. He committed suicide in 1972.

10. Tanizaki Jun'ichiro (Shunkinsho)

In many of the works of Tanizaki Jun'ichiro, idolisation of the female sex is a very powerful theme. As can be seen in

れた「ナオミ」のようなタイプは，明治時代（1868—1911）の作家たちには想像もつかない*産物だろう。

しかし同じ女性崇拝という立場をとりながら，『春琴抄』に描かれた春琴と佐助の物語は，美しくまねできないほど完全な愛の姿を私たちに見せる。

美しい盲目の琴の*師，春琴と*奉公人，佐助の愛。春琴37歳のある夜，何者かが彼女の顔に*熱湯を注いだ。佐助は醜い顔を見られることを恐れた春琴の気持ちを察して，自分の両眼を針で突いて悲しみに応じた。

「お師匠様，わたしは*めしいになりました」
「佐助，それはほんとうか」

この小説は作者が関東大震災[1]（1923）後，関西に移住し，大阪を舞台に描かれている。

谷崎潤一郎（1866—1965）の代表作は『細雪』『痴人の愛』『卍』である。

VOCABULARY　*Suhai*: veneration, adoration, idolisation　*Kannoteki*: carnal, lascivious　*Sanbutsu*: product　*Shi*: master, mistress (title given to teacher of some traditional Japanese performing art)　*Hokonin*: servant, serving man, apprentice　*Netto*: boiling water　*Meshii*: blind

196　Ⅷ．日本の文学

Chijin no Ai ("A Fool's Love"), for example, the kind of woman typified by Naomi, who seems to be the product of masculine sensual desires, would have been inconceivable to writers of the Meiji Period (1868–1911).

Nevertheless, although *Shunkinsho* ("The Story of Shunkin") is also written from the same point of view, as far as the veneration of women is concerned, the story of Shunkin and Sasuke that it describes, gives us an example of perfect love in a form that is beyond imitation.

The theme is the love of the beautiful but blind Shunkin, a teacher of the koto, and the serving man, Sasuke. When Shunkin was thirty-seven, someone threw boiling water into her face one evening. Realising that Shunkin is fearful of him seeing her disfigurement, Sasuke responds to her grief by piercing both his own eyes with a needle.

"Mistress, I've become blind".
"Sasuke, are you telling me the truth?"

The novel is set in Osaka after the author had moved there following the Great Kanto Earthquake of 1923.

Principal works of Tanizaki Jun'ichiro (1866–1965) are *Sasame Yuki* ("The Makioka Sisters"), *Chijin no Ai* ("A Fool's Love"), *Manji* ("Swastika"), etc.

注

1. 関東大震災
 1923年9月1日，マグニチュード8の大地震があり，東京だけでも死者6万人，経済上の損害65億円と推定され，このため経済界は大混乱となった。

11. 三島由紀夫

　1970年11月の三島由紀夫（1925—1970）の死が，どうしても歴史上の一コマだとは思えない。居間のテレビには*軍服で*鉢巻き姿の彼が自衛隊のバルコニーで演説していた。アナウンサーは狂気のようにしゃべりまくり，三島は*割腹自殺によって一生の幕を閉じた。

　第二次世界大戦後，青年の代弁者として，小説，戯曲，評論と活躍し時代の花形だった三島，ボディービルをしたり，映画に出演したりして話題をまいた三島，そして最後には天皇制を審美的に理想化し，フィクションと現実との境界線を踏み越えてあの世にいってしまった。彼の作風を好きな人も嫌いな人も強烈な生き方は，非常に心に残るだろう。

　代表作は『金閣寺』『仮面の告白』『宴のあと』などの長編，『鹿鳴館』などの戯曲，『道成寺』などを収めた『近代能楽集』がある。

NOTES

1. Great Kanto Earthquake: The earthquake that occurred on September 1, 1923, with a magnitude of eight on the Japanese scale. In Tokyo, alone, 60,000 people died and the cost of the damage was estimated at ¥6,500,000,000. The Japanese economy was thrown into confusion as a result.

11. Mishima Yukio

It is hard to believe that the death of Mishima Yukio (1925–1970) in November, 1970 is of great historical significance. He appeared on our living room television sets dressed in his military uniform with a hachimaki around his forehead as he delivered a speech standing on the balcony of the headquarters of the Self Defence Forces. The announcer screamed hysterically as Mishima then went on to end his own life, committing suicide by ritual disembowelment.

After the Second World War Mishima, as a spokesman for the young, became a celebrity of the age through his many activities as novelist, playwright and critic. He also attracted much attention for his body building and film appearances. He went on to idealise and beautify the concept of the Emperor system before crossing the dividing line between fiction and reality in his ultimate death. Whether they admire his writings or not, there is no doubt that there are many who remain impressed by the intensity with which he lived.

VOCABULARY *Gunpuku:* military uniform *Hachimaki:* a cloth band tied around the forehead *Kappuku jisatsu:* suicide by ritual disembowelment

Mishima's principal works include the novels *Kinkakuji* ("The Temple of the Golden Pavilion"), *Kamen no Kokuhaku* ("Confessions of a Mask"), *Utage no Ato* ("After the Banquet") and a number of plays including *Rokumeikan* ("The Deer Cry Pavilion"). He also wrote *Dojoji* ("Dojo Temple"), one of a set of modern Noh dramas.

IX. 日本経済の特質

1. 高度成長

　日本は敗戦¹によって, 経済力は*壊滅に近い状態になった。そして経済が*回復するのは, 1950年に起こった朝鮮戦争の特需²によってである。1955年以降, 日本経済は高度成長の段階に入る。その後オイルショックによって1974年, 戦後はじめて経済成長率がマイナスを記録するまでの約20年間は年平均10％以上の高度成長を続けた。1968年にＧＮＰ³は合衆国に次いで世界第2位となり, 「経済大国」として*注目されるようになった。

　この時期に日本は, *先進的な技術の*導入によって重化学工業化した。これを可能にしたのは, 戦争によって古い設備の大半が消滅していたこと, 新技術をマスターできる良質の労働力が存在したこと, *設備投資を可能にした国民の高い*貯蓄に対する性向があったことなどである。

VOCABULARY　　*Kaimetsu:* destruction, annihilation　　*Kaifuku:* recovery　　*Chumoku:* attention, notice　　*Senshinteki:* progressive, advanced　　*Donyu:* introduction　　*Setsubitoshi:* investment in equipment　　*Chochiku:* savings

IX. Characteristics of the Japanese Economy

1. High-speed Growth

The result of defeat in war, Japan's economic strength was all but destroyed. The recovery of the economy began in 1950 with the supply of special procurements for the Korean War. After 1955, the economy entered a period of high-speed growth achieving an annual rate of over 10%. This continued for nearly twenty years until 1974 when, for the first time after the war, minus economic growth was recorded. It was in 1968 that Japan attracted attention as an economic giant when its GNP was second highest in the world after the United States of America.

During this period, Japan became a heavy scientific and industrial nation, the result of the introduction of advanced technology. This was made possible by the destruction during the war of most of the old plants and equipment; the existence of a good quality labour force able to master new techniques; and the people's high level of personal savings that allowed investment in new equipment to take place.

注───────────────────────
1. 敗戦　　第二次世界大戦（1939—1945）。
2. 特需　　特別な需要（一般に，在日米軍が日本で調達する物資についていう）。
3. GNP　　国民総生産。

2. 中小企業

「大企業の下で，*下請けの仕事をする」これが今まで私たちがもっていた中小企業のイメージではないでしょうか。しかし日本人の生活が豊かになり，消費者の求めるものが質的に変化を始め，中小企業の活躍の場も広がってきました。

たとえば，他人とは違う個性的なものが欲しい（*需要の*多様化），デザインに飽きたので買い換える（短サイクル化），こういう要求に大規模な設備をもつ大企業では，*応じきれない部分があるのです。そこで中小企業の*機動性と*創造性が生きてくるのです。

現在エレクトロニクスの分野などでは，*独自の製品を開発し，世界のシェアーの半分以上を占めている中小企業がいくつもあります。こうなると，大企業が*頭を下げてその製品を買いにくるようになります。大企業の下請けというイメージとはだいぶ違いますね。

そして海外に輸出される製品の40％以上が中小企業によって作り出されています。中小企業が，日本の経済を支えているといっても言い過ぎではないでしょう。しかし，事業所数わずか1％の

NOTES

1. The Second World War.
2. Supplies of materials for the American army in Japan.
3. Gross National Product.

2. The Small- and Medium-Sized Businesses

Until now, the image of small- and medium-sized businesses has been as subcontractors to major companies. However, with the affluence that has come to the lives of the Japanese people and with the changes in the demands of consumers in relation to quality, the area of activity of the small- and medium-sized businesses has widened considerably.

For example, when a request comes for a product with more individuality to distinguish it from other people's (diversification of demand). Or when the same type of product is wanted but with a different design (because people have grown tired of the old design—the short cycle phenomenon), big organisations with large-scale facilities often have difficulty complying with such demands. It is then that the adaptability and creativity of the smaller company come into play.

At present in the field of electronics, there are countless examples of small- and medium-sized companies that have developed original products and now have over half the world's

大企業と99%を占める中小企業との間には，賃金や労働条件に大きな格差があります。このへんのところをどう解決していくかが，日本の経済のこれからにも，大きく影響してくるでしょう。

円高の問題，*市場開放など中小企業にとってはこれから苦しい時代になりそうです。でも，技術力を向上させ，ぜひこの時代を乗り切ってほしいものです。

VOCABULARY *Shitauke:* subcontractor *Juyo:* demand *Tayoka:* diversification *Ojikirenai:* be unable to respond to, comply with *Kidosei:* adaptability, manoeuvrability *Sozosei:* creativity *Dokuji:* original *Atama o sageru:* be deferential to *Ichiba kaiho:* opening up of markets

3. 農業と食糧の問題

日本の食糧*自給率は，年々低下してきている。それは1955年の高度成長期に始まった。政府は*能率が悪い上に，費用のかかる国内の農産物を保護するよりは，安い外国の食糧を輸入した方

share. When representatives from big business come with the intention of buying these products, their behaviour is suitably deferential. The image of the small- or medium-sized business as nothing more than a subcontractor is now very different.

In addition, more than 40% of manufactured goods exported abroad are produced by such smaller firms. In view of this it is no exaggeration to say that the smaller- and medium-sized businesses are supporting the nation's economy. But between large corporations, which constitute only 1% of the total number of business operations and small- and medium-sized businesses which make up 99%, there is a tremendous difference regarding labour conditions and the possibility of financial loans. The way this area of difficulty is dealt with will have a great influence on the Japanese economy from now on.

With the problems of the high rate of the yen and the opening up of markets, small- and medium-sized firms seem to be entering a period of great difficulty. It is to be hoped that, by putting their technical skills first, they will be able to ride out the storm.

3. Agriculture and Food

Japan's rate of self-sufficiency is annually becoming lower, a phenomenon that began in 1955 during the period of high economic growth. That this has come about is the result not

が得だと考えたからだ。たとえば，日本人の好むてんぷらそばを例にとれば，原料のそば粉，小麦粉，油，えび，しょう油，砂糖，すべて輸入品であり，日本産は「職人の腕だけだ」と悪口を言われる。現在の自給率は30％程度，また農業に就いている人の数は全体の8.1％にすぎない。

日本人の主食である米は，1970年以来政府が生産調整を行っている。これは収穫率が上昇し政府が米を農民から高く買い，消費者に安く売るという制度を採ったことなどから，*生産過剰になったからである。

もし世界的な*食糧不足が起こったり，外国が農産物の輸出を制限したりすると，食糧輸入国である日本は，たちまち困ることになるだろう。

VOCABULARY　　*Jikyuritsu:* rate of self-sufficiency　　*Noritsu ga warui (yoi):* inefficient (efficient)　　*Seisan kajo:* overproduction　　*Shokuryo busoku:* lack of food

4. 漁業——乱獲200カイリ

日本人にとって*ごちそうといえばマグロの*刺身，これは200トン以上の大型船が*遠洋に進出してとってきたものであり，その漁獲高は日本の漁業中第一位である。

そしてお弁当のおかずといえば昔は塩ザケがその代表だった。

only of government inefficiency but also of the policy of preferring to import cheap foodstuffs from abroad rather than protect expensive, domestic agricultural produce. To take tempura, a favorite with the Japanese, as an example, all the ingredients—flour, baking powder prawns, soy source and sugar—are imported, so it can be said, sarcastically, that "Made in Japan" applies only to the skills of the workers. The actual rate of self-sufficiency is 30% and the percentage of the work force engaged in agriculture is only 8.1%.

As far as rice, the staple food of the Japanese, is concerned, the government has been carrying out a policy of regulated production. This is a system whereby the government buys the rice from farmers at a high price and sells it cheaply to consumers. Add to this the increase in crop yield, and the result is over production.

If a world shortage of food were to occur and foreign countries limited their exports of agricultural goods, Japan would soon find itself in a very difficult situation.

4. Fishing Industry (200 Mile Limit)

Something the Japanese enjoy eating very much is tuna sashimi. The tuna are caught in ocean going trawlers of over 200 tons and the total production is the highest in the fishing industry.

しかし乱獲によって沿岸近海の魚資源はなくなりつつある。200カイリ[1]以内のソ連沿岸で、魚をとれなくなった日本漁船は、サケ、マスを外洋で*漁獲する技術を開発した。しかしこれも、外洋を*回遊するサケ、マスにも*母川国(ぼせんこく)にその権利があるという主張が強くなっている。外洋で*根こそぎとってしまえば、自分たちの生まれ故郷の川へ帰って行くサケやマスが少なくなるのは当然で母川国の主張もうなずける。

サケも段々庶民には手の届かない魚となるかもしれない。

VOCABULARY　　*Gochiso:* something people enjoy eating, a treat　　*Sashimi:* fresh fish served uncooked in thin slices and eaten with soy sauce and wasabi (Japanese horse radish)　　*Enyo:* the open sea(s)　　*Gyokaku suru:* catch, haul of fish　　*Kaiyu suru:* migrate (of fish)　　*Bosenkoku:* state of origin of anadromous stock　　*Nekosogi:* exhaustively

注
1. 200カイリ（200カイリ漁業専管水域）
   沿岸国が領海（一般に12カイリ）を越えて、200カイリにわたり、漁業の資源を保存するために、外国船による漁獲を規制する水域。

Then there is salmon which, roasted and salted, used to be a part of the average bento or lunch box. Indiscriminate fishing in coastal waters, however, destroys stocks. But as Japanese fishing boats are no longer able to operate off the Russian coast because of the two hundred mile limit, techniques have been developed to catch salmon and sea trout in the open sea. It is now being insisted, however, that the rights to the fish that migrate to the open seas lie with the state of origin of anadromous stock. If salmon and trout are fished exhaustively in the open seas, the numbers returning to their native rivers will gradually decrease. In view of this the insistence on their rights by the countries affected is understandable.

Salmon may become too expensive for ordinary Japanese people before too long.

NOTES

1. 200 mile limit (200 mile exclusive fishing zone): A country's territorial waters are extended from twelve to two hundred miles to protect fishing resources and to control the activities of foreign fishing fleets.

X. コンピュータ

1. コンピュータ社会

　私たちの生活はコンピュータのおかげで，このごろ大変便利になってきた。

　旅行に行きたい*とする。指定券を買いに，「みどりの窓口」[1]に行く。「みどりの窓口」はコンピュータによってオンライン化[2]されているから，*空席があればどこの窓口でもすぐ買える。

　そして旅に出る。現金はそんなに持って出る必要はない。たとえば東京の支店に*預金口座のある場合，北海道の札幌にいても，南の九州にいても現金を引き出すことができる。これは*ほとんどの*都市銀行が専用の*通信回線を使って，北海道から沖縄までひとつのコンピュータシステムを作りあげたからだ。どの銀行のどの支店でも現金が引き出せる。それも*即座に引き出せる。以前には考えられなかったことだ。

　しかしコンピュータだって機械だから，*故障することもある。そんな時は日本全国でお金が引き出せないという，困ったことになる。もっとも，そんな話は聞いたことがないから，あまり心配する必要はなさそうだ。

　その他にも，電気・ガス・水道料金の*請求書，給料の計算書，私たちの*身近なところで，コンピュータからはじき出されたも

X. Computer

1. Computer Society

Computers have made some aspects of modern life much easier in recent times.

For example, suppose you want to take a trip. You go to the "Green Counter" to buy a ticket for a reserved seat. The Green Counter has an online link to a central computer and if there are tickets still available, you can buy one to wherever you want to go at any JR station with a Green Counter.

Now you set off on your trip. You don't have to take a lot of cash with you. Let's say you have a savings account at a branch of a bank in Tokyo. Even if you go all the way up to Sapporo in Hokkaido, or down south to Kyushu, you can readily withdraw cash from a bank there. This is because the major banks are linked on a dedicated communications network that forms a single computer system from Hokkaido to Okinawa. You can withdraw money from any bank on the system. No need to wait in front of a bank counter. Something that would never have been possible just a few years ago.

Now, a computer is a machine, so sometimes it breaks down.

のがたくさんある。学校の先生は,「コンピュータのおかげで,試験や成績の*分析が大変*楽になった」と言われるし,*マスコミ業界の人は「ラジオ・テレビの番組編成,*選挙速報,新聞の*紙面制作が正確に短時間でできるようになりました」と言われる。コンピュータの利用について書こうと思ったら,一冊の本が必要なくらいだ。今後もあらゆる分野で,コンピュータは活躍するようになるだろう。

VOCABULARY　　～*to suru:* let's say　　*Kuseki:* available seats　*Yokin koza:* savings account　　*Toshi ginko:* major banks　*Tsushin kaisen:* communications network　　*Sokuzani:* immediately　*Kosho:* breakdown　*Seikyusho:* bill　*Mijika:* close　*Bunseki:* analysis　*Raku ni naru:* become easier　　*Masukomi gyokai:* media people　　*Senkyo sokuho:* election report　　*Shimen seisaku:* newspaper production

注

1. みどりの窓口
   乗る日の1か月前から,指定券の発売をしたり,遠距離の乗車券などの発売をする駅の窓口。
2. オンライン化
   端末装置が駅の窓口に置かれ,客が来た時には,中央のコンピュータに照会して,空席があれば発売するという方法。

If that happens it would then be impossible to withdraw money anywhere in the country; an intolerable situation. Well, it has never happened, and it is not likely to, so it does not seem to be something worth worrying about.

Bills for electricity, gas and water fees, salary slips and many other such forms that we have to deal with every day are now printed up by computers. School teachers say "Computers make analysis of test results and student performance much easier." Media people say "Editing radio and television programmes, election reports, and preparing newspaper copy can now be done faster with no loss in accuracy." They are certainly very much appreciated in many fields of activity, and computers will certainly be used much more in the future. Clearly, one cannot really cover a topic like computers in society in anything less than an entire book.

NOTES

1. Green Counter: This is the JR counter where tickets are sold for reserved seats up to one month before the date of use, and where long-distance train tickets are sold.
2. Terminals are installed at the ticket offices of every JR station. When a customer asks for a ticket stating the destination, date and time, the booking clerk sends a query to the central computer. The response is returned immediately and if there is a seat available, he can sell it to the customer.

2. ソフトウェア, ハードウェア

コンピュータは装置(ハードウェア)とプログラム(ソフトウェア)の2つのものの働きで動く。

コンピュータは、金属などでできた機械そのものだけではなんの*役にも立たない。そこでコンピュータのすべき動作を*指示したプログラムを作っておいて、これに従ってコンピュータを働かせる。コンピュータは、考えられないような速さでこのプログラムを読み、その指示のとおりに実行していく。この動作を記したプログラムというソフトウェアが、大変*重要になってくる。

最近では、ハードウェアは半導体技術の進歩[1]によって、値段が大変安くなってきた。パソコンなら1セット20万円くらいで買える。これでも*記憶容量は6万バイト以上(6万字)と10年前の1000万円近いコンピュータに*匹敵する。

ところがソフトウェアは人が作るものだから、コストは*人件費にかかり、値段はむしろ高くなってきている。このためにコンピュータのコストのうち、ソフトウェアの*占める部分がだんだん高くなっている。小型のコンピュータでは、ハードウェアよりも、ソフトウェアの*価格の方が高くなることも珍しくない。

VOCABULARY　*Yaku ni tatsu (tatanai):* useful (useless)　*Shiji:* indicate　*Juyo na:* important　*Kioku yoryo:* memory capacity　*Hitteki suru:* match　*Jinkenhi:* personnel costs　*Shimeru:* occupy　*Kakaku:* cost

注
1. 半導体技術の進歩

2. Software and Hardware

The two components of a computer are the basic electronics, called hardware, and the programs written by human programmers, called software. If computers consisted of nothing but the metal electronics, they would be useless. They need the programs to direct their operations; these are what make the computers function as they are intended to. The computer reads the programs at speeds faster than thought, and executes the operations exactly as specified. Efficient software is indispensable.

Recent advances in semiconductor technology have resulted in dramatic decreases in the cost of hardware. You can now buy a personal computer for just ¥200,000 and it will have a memory capacity of more than 60,000 bytes (i.e., 60,000 characters), matching that of a computer that would have cost 10 million yen only ten years ago.

Software is written by people, and as such the cost comes under personnel costs. Consequently, in contrast to hardware, the cost of software has been increasing, and with it the share of the cost of a computer occupied by software has gradually increased. In a small-scale computer, it is not unusual for the cost of software to exceed that of the hardware.

NOTES
1. Large-scale integration (LSI) semiconductor technology began

1970年以降ＬＳＩ（大規模集積回路）がコンピュータに使用されるようになった。これはトランジスタにすると数万個から数十万個分が，数ミリ四方の半導体の中に組み込まれたもの。この半導体１個でコンピュータの頭脳の働きをすることができる。

3. IBM と日本製コンピュータ

ＩＢＭは，コンピュータの世界を常にリードしてきた会社であり，アメリカ国内で70％，*世界市場ではほとんどの国で50％以上のシェアをもっているといわれる。

ところで，日本のコンピュータ*開発は，アメリカに比べて10年は遅れて出発した，というのが*常識になっている。政府はコンピュータ，特にソフトウェアに関しては，*貿易の自由化を許可しないで，国産コンピュータに，*徹底した*保護政策[1]をとってきた。また大型コンピュータやソフトウェアのために使われた政府資金は何百億円だそうである。こうした*強力な保護のおかげで，日本ではＩＢＭのものに匹敵，中には*勝るものすら開発できるようになった。ところが高度なソフトウェアについては，とても追いつけないだろうという意見が*有力である。

VOCABULARY　　*Sekai shijo:* world market　　*Kaihatsu:* development　　*Joshiki:* common knowledge　　*Boeki no jiyuka:* freedom of trade　　*Tettei shita:* rigorous　　*Hogo seisaku:* protection policy　　*Kyoryoku na:* powerful　　*Masaru:* excel　　*Yuryoku na:* generally accepted

218 X. コンピュータ

to be used in computers in 1970. Large-scale integration means that from ten thousand to several million transistors are integrated on a semiconductor chip of only a few millimeters in area. Just one of these chips, called a microprocessor, can be used to run a computer.

3. IBM and Japanese Computers

IBM has long been the world leader in the computer industry. The company is said to hold 70% of the market for computers within the United States and more than 50% of the market in most other countries.

However, it is now common knowledge that Japan started developing computers about ten years after America. The government did not allow free trade in computers, in particular in software, and domestically produced computers were subject to a *rigorous protection policy*. They have also spent several billion yen on development of software and mainframe computers. This powerful protection and support has borne fruit. Japan is now capable of developing computers that match or even surpass those of IBM. Although it is generally accepted that there is no chance of Japan overtaking them in the field of advanced software.

注
1. 保護政策
   1957年に制定された「電子工業振興臨時措置法(しんこうりんじそちほう)」制定以来国産コンピュータの保護政策がとられた。

4. コンピュータとプライバシー

　現代のようなコンピュータ社会で，私たちがいつも*自覚しておかなければいけないのは，「コンピュータを動かすのは人間」ということだろう。

　*税務署が私たちの*所得を*管理し，*警察が自動車の*免許を管理し，市役所や区役所が，*住民基本台帳を管理している。管理しているといっても，あくまでもコンピュータは道具なのであって，それを利用するのは人間なのだ。現在では住民基本台帳に所得，税金，その他を加えようとしている。こうすることによって私たちのプライバシーは*行政に握られることになる。

　まして国民総背番号制[1]になり，個人の情報がまとめてコンピュータに*記憶されるとしたら，どういうことになるだろうか。所得，*財産，*犯罪歴，社会*福祉関係や*戸籍関係など，*一定のコード（符号）のもとに情報を集め，それを必要に応じて取り出すというのはコンピュータにとってなんでもないことなので，個人情報は完全に行政によって管理されるようになるだろう。もし再び日本に徴兵制がとられるとしたら国民総背番号制は，その効果をもっとも*発揮するだろう。

　コンピュータ，特に大型の*高性能なものは，*官公庁や一部の

NOTES
1. The "Electronics Industry Promotion Provisional Measure Law" enacted in 1957 initiated the policy of protection for domestically produced computers.

4. Computers and Privacy

One point we must never lose sight of in all this enthusiasm for computers is that "computers are run by human beings."

The tax authorities check our incomes, the police issue and check automobile licenses, the city and ward offices control residents' registration. Now they use computers for all of this work. At the moment there is a movement in Japan to combine all this information—residents registration, income, tax, etc.—into one vast information bank. This would give these various authorities control over our private lives.

Moreover, if this leads to an identity number being given to every citizen, and all the information on every individual being stored in a computer under this number, where will it all lead? Information on income and property, criminal records, welfare records, and residents' registration data would all be collected under a fixed code (identification number). It could be easily retrieved as needed giving the authorities complete control over the data on every citizen. And if another conscription law is enacted in Japan, then these identification numbers

大企業しか利用できない。*特定の人だけが大きなコンピュータを使い，情報を*独占していく，そしてその*反面，個人のプライバシーは*犯され，コンピュータを利用できる人とできない人との*差がどんどん広がっていくという恐れもある。

　コンピュータが今後どのように使われていくのか，私たちには*監視する*義務があるのではないだろうか。

VOCABULARY　　*Jikaku suru:* realize　　*Zeimusho:* tax office　*Shotoku:* income　　*Kanri suru:* oversee　　*Keisatsu:* police　　*Menkyo:* license　　*Jumin kihon daicho:* resident registration　　*Gyosei:* authorities　　*Kioku:* memorize　　*Shisan:* property　　*Hanzaireki:* criminal record　　*Fukushi:* welfare　　*Koseki:* residents' registration data　　*Ittei no:* specified　　*Hakki suru:* show　　*Koseino:* advanced functions　　*Kankocho:* government and municipal offices　*Tokutei no:* specified　　*Dokusen suru:* monopolize　　*Hanmen:* in contrast　　*Okasareru:* be damaged (not be damaged)　　*Sa:* difference　　*Kanshi suru:* supervine　　*Gimu:* obligation

注
1. 国民総背番号制
   国民のひとりひとりに番号をつけ，その番号を使って，政府が全国民のデータをコンピュータで管理しようとするやり方。

would surely take on an ominous significance.

Large-scale computers, in particular the advanced function mainframe machines, can only be used by the government and municipal offices and the big companies. Only specified persons have access to them, giving them a monopoly of information. This will surely damage individual privacy. There is also the problem of a widening gulf between those who can and those who cannot use computers.

How will computers be used in the future? Don't you agree that this is an issue which we are obliged to consider very carefully?

NOTES

1. The idea of giving every single person in Japan a number which will be used to maintain computerized information on the general populace, so that the government can keep it under surveillance and control.

XI. ロボット

　日本は「ロボット王国」といわれている。ロボットの生産は，川崎重工業，日立などの大企業を含む130もの企業が*従事し，1990年には一兆円の生産高に*達するといわれている。

1. 産業用ロボット

　世界の産業用ロボットの7割が大工場から小さな町工場に至るまで，日本のあらゆる場所で働いている。

　価格は平均350万円と，中年の労働者の*年給とほぼ同じである。それではロボットが人間より有利な点はなんであろうか。*作業が正確，休まず働く，製品の品質を安定させる，*つらい仕事を文句も言わずにする。たとえば，*重量物を扱うこと，*単調な仕事を続けること，危険な仕事，騒音の激しい仕事など。これらは仕事のなり手が少ないことから，ロボットが使われることが多い。

　日本でロボットが*普及した原因を考えてみると，労働者の教育水準が高く，*技術革新を*受け入れやすかったこと，日本の*失業率が低く，労働力が不足していたことなどが考えられる。*今

XI. Robots

Japan is sometimes called the Robot Kingdom. There are now no less than 130 companies producing robots in Japan, including industrial giants like Kawasaki Heavy Industries and Hitachi. Estimates indicate that robot production will reach one trillion yen by the year 1990.

1. Industrial Robots

Robots are at work all over the country, from the largest industrial plants to the smallest local factories. Seven out of ten robots in the world today are working in Japan.

An industrial robot will cost somewhere around three and a half million yen, just about the same as the annual income of a middle-aged male worker in Japan. So what are the advantages of using robots over human workers? Well, for one thing they perform their tasks accurately and continuously, that is to say they do not need to rest, which stabilizes product quality. Robots perform unpleasant work such as moving and lifting heavy weights, or monotonous, repetitive tasks without complaining. They can also operate under severe noise levels

後も*産業用ロボットは国内需要ばかりでなく輸出産業として,伸びていくと思われる。

VOCABULARY　　*Juji suru:* engage in　　*Tassuru:* reach　　*Nenkkyu:* annual income　　*Sagyo:* task　　*Tsurai sigoto:* unpleasant work　　*Juryobutsu:* heavy weights　　*Tancho no:* monotonous　　*Fukyu shita:* spread　　*Gijutsu kakushin:* new developments in technology　　*Ukeire yasui (nikui) koto:* readiness (unwillingness) to accept　　*Shitsugyo ritsu:* unemployment rate　　*Kongo:* in the future　　*Sangyo yo:* industrial

2. ロボット導入のよいこと, 悪いこと

　人間にとってつらい仕事をロボットがしてくれる——これはまったくすばらしいことだ。それに*経営者にとっても, ロボットを使うことで*コストが下がり, 生産量が増えるのだから, これからもどんどんロボットを使うことになるだろう。

　しかしロボット*導入がいいとばかりとは限らない。ロボットは機械だから, 言いつけられた仕事をいかに忠実に, 効果的に行うにしても*手加減することを知らない。ロボットの腕にはさまれて死んだ作業員もいるし, *電磁波によって*暴走したロボットが死亡事故を起こしたこともある。ロボット導入による一番*深刻な問題は, 企業内の*配置転換などで, 余剰人員が生じて, 失業問題にまで発展していくことだろう。*熟練工が1時間かかる*精密加工をロボットが10分間でできるからといって, 慣れ親し

or under dangerous working conditions. Robots are often used for these kinds of work because few human workers are prepared to do them.

Let's take a look at the factors which promoted the spread of robots in Japan. The principle reasons are the high standard of education of the workforce and their readiness to accept new technological developments, the low unemployment rate, and the shortage of labor. It seems that in the future robots will not only be produced to meet the domestic demand, but robot exports from Japan will also increase.

2. Robots Good and Bad

Using robots to perform work that is unpleasant for human beings is surely something to be welcomed. Employing robots also has advantages for managers. Robots can reduce production costs and increase productivity. These are important considerations and they suggest that the number of robots in use will probably increase in the future.

However, there are also problems associated with the introduction of robots. They are, after all, machines, and however responsive and effective they may be in their assigned tasks, there are many things they are not sensitive to. Workers have been crushed to death in the arms of robots, and there are cases of robots being driven out of control by electromagnetic

んだ職場を追われるのは悔しいに違いない。

　*労働省の調べでは，こうして仕事を失っていくのは40歳以上の人が多いとのこと。つまり，この年代になると，なかなか新しい技術に*適応できないからだろう。

　こうして考えてみると，ロボットがつらい仕事を引き受けてくれると喜んでいるうちに，人間の仕事が減って職を失うことになる。労働者たちがうかうかしていられない事態が起こることは十分に考えられる。

VOCABULARY　*Keieisha:* management　*Kosuto no sagari (agari):* cost reduction (increase)　*Donyu:* introduction　*Tekagen:* consideration　*Denjiha:* electromagnetic radiation　*Boso suru:* run out of control　*Sinkoku na mondai:* serious problems　*Haichi tenkan:* redesign of layout　*Jukurenko:* skilled operative　*Seimitsu kako:* precision processing　*Rodosho:* the Ministry of Labor　*Tekio:* adaptation

3.　中小企業とロボット

　中小企業にも ロボットの導入は*急速に進んでいる。 どうしてだろうか。よくいわれているように，*技能労働者の*不足分を，ロボットが*補っているのだろうか。そうとばかりはいえない気がする。日本の大企業は「*国際競争力」を*強化するために，*下

radiation and killing workers. These may be isolated cases, but the most general and serious problems range from the extensive redesign of plant layout that may be required to accommodate them to the unemployment problems they create. When one considers that it takes a robot only ten minutes to execute the precision processing that usually takes a skilled operative one hour to perform, it is clear that there are bound to be many difficulties in developing a friendly working atmosphere for the human workers.

According to studies by the Ministry of Labor, many workers over the age of forty will be put out of work by robots because once past forty people are much less capable of adapting to the new technologies.

Thus, while robots taking over performance of unpleasant, dangerous and difficult tasks from human operatives represents a real improvement in working conditions, the reduction and even complete loss of work or employment is surely a very serious issue for the workers.

3. Robots in Small- and Medium-sized Businesses

The introduction of robots has also progressed rapidly in small- and medium-sized firms. It is often said, that the reason for this is that robots have to be used to compensate for the shortage of skilled workers. But one has the feeling that this

請け企業を利用してきた。1986年の円高により，輸出競争力の落ちた自動車・電機産業などは下請けである中小企業に，もっと*きびしい要求を突き付けている。生産コストを下げること，品質を*均一化させること，*納期を*短縮させることなど。こうなると，中小企業は苦しい*経営の中から，ロボットを導入*せざるを得なくなる。「うちの会社だけロボットを入れないと，*つぶれてしまう」と考えるからだ。

一般の労働組合はロボットの問題をあまり*重視していないようだが，労働者の失業につながる問題なので，ロボット導入について，もっと議論する必要があるだろう。

VOCABULARY　*Kyusoku:* rapid　*Gino rodosha:* skilled worker　*Fusoku bun:* shortage　*Oginau:* compensate for　*Kokusai kyoso ryoku:* international competitiveness　*Kyoka suru:* strengthen　*Shitauke kigyo:* subcontractor　*Kakoku na:* severe　*Kin-itsu ka saseru:* stabilize　*Noki:* delivery times　*Tanshuku saseru:* shorten　*Sezaru o enai:* be forced to　*Tsubureru:* go under　*Jushi suru:* regard seriously

4. ロボットの種類と用途

日本産業用ロボット工業会の*定義によれば，ロボットは次の6種類に分けられる。

① マニュアル・マニピュレータ

手で*操るものという意味。*原子炉や*潜水船で使われ，つかんだり，動かしたりする。つまり手の代わりをするだけの道具で

cannot be all there is to say on the matter. Large Japanese companies have long been using subcontractors extensively in order to strengthen their "international competitiveness." The increase in the value of the yen in 1986 has meant that the firms whose export competitiveness has fallen, such as those in areas like automobiles and electrical equipment, are now making much more severe demands on their subcontractors, which are small- and medium-sized companies. Demands such as reducing production costs, stabilizing product quality, and shortening delivery times. These factors all combine to force the difficult decisions which the managers of the small- and medium-sized companies have to make when introducing robots. They think that "If we try to stand alone and refuse to introduce robots, we'll go under."

The trade unions do not seem to regard robots as a serious problem, but their use is clearly linked to unemployment, so surely there is a need for more discussion of this issue.

4. Varieties of Robots and Their Applications

According to the current definitions of industrial robots in Japan, robots can be classified into the following six types.

(1) Manual manipulators

As the name suggest, these robots are manually controlled. They are used in nuclear reactors and submarines, and can be

ある。

② **固定シーケンス・ロボット**

このロボットは動力を使うが決まった動作しかしない。*価格も安いので中小企業でも使いやすい。

③ **可変シーケンス・ロボット**

一定のことを*連続して行うが、その動作も変えることができる。

④ **プレイバック・ロボット**

マイコン（マイクロ・コンピュータ）つきのロボットで、人間が教えたとおりの動作を繰り返す。

⑤ **数値制御ロボット**

カードやテープなどに情報を入れておき、ロボットに*指示を与える。*工作機械などに使われる。

⑥ **知能ロボット**

人間のように感じたり、物事を*認識したりすることができる。センサ[1]から受けた情報に応じて、*最適な動作を自動的に行うロボットである。

VOCABULARY　　*Teigi:* definition　　*Ayatsuru:* manipulate
Genshi ro: nuclear reactor　　*Sensui sen:* submarine　　*Kakaku:* price　　*Renzoku shite:* continuously　　*Shiji:* instruction　　*Kosaku kikai:* machine tools　　*Ninshiki suru:* recognize　　*Saiteki na:* optimal

注
1. センサ
   温度、圧力、湿度などを知る機能をもった装置のこと。

worked with ease by human operators. Thus, they are simply tools that replace the human hand.

(2) Fixed sequence robots

These robots are independently mobile, but they perform only limited and strictly defined operations. Fixed sequence robots are relatively cheap so they are often used in small- and medium-sized companies.

(3) Variable sequence robots

Performing specified tasks continuously, the sequence of operations specified for these robots can be changed.

(4) Playback robots

Playback robots are based on microcomputers, and they repeat sequences of operations specified by human operators.

(5) Numerically controlled robots

These sophisticated robots accept instructions from data written on computer cards or magnetic tape. They are used in such applications as machine tools.

(6) Intelligent robots

Intelligent robots are so-called because they can think and recognize things just as human beings do, automatically performing the optimal sequence of operations based on the data they acquire from their own sensors.

NOTES

1. Sensors: Precision electronic instruments capable of registering such quantities as temperatures, pressures and humidity levels.

佐々木瑞枝（ささき・みずえ）
 1942年，京都に生まる。
 日大文理学部英文学科卒。米国カリフォルニア州 Golden State Univ. 大学院比較言語学専攻。
 アメリカンスクール，横浜国立大学の講師を経て，現在山口大学教授。英文朝日のコラムニスト。

Mizue Sasaki was born in Kyoto in 1942 and graduated from Nihon Univ. (BA) and Golden State Univ. (MA) in California majoring in Comparative Language Studies.

She has taught Japanese language at the American School in Japan and Yokohama National University, and is currently a professor at Yamaguchi National University. She is also a columnist for the Asahi Evening News.

昭和62年9月25日　初版発行
昭和63年4月1日　3刷発行

日本事情 JAPAN à la carte
©

著者　佐々木　瑞枝

発行者　株式会社 北星堂書店

代表者　山本雅三

発行所　株式会社 北星堂書店
101　東京都千代田区神田神保町1-46
電話 (03) 294-3301　FAX (03) 294-3305

印刷・製本　住友出版印刷

定価1800円

落丁・乱丁本はお取替致します
本書の内容の一部あるいは全部を無断で複写複製
することは法律で認められた場合を除き著作権お
よび出版社の権利の侵害となりますのでその場合
には予め小社の承諾を得て下さい。